Martha Schwartz

Recycling Spaces

Curating Urban Evolution

Recycling Spaces

The Work of Martha Schwartz Partners

Curating Urban Evolution

Emily Waugh

ORO edition

Table of Contents

Urban Effects and the Recent Work of Martha Schwartz

Charles Waldheim

The recent work of Martha Schwartz Partners illustrates a transformation in the practice of landscape architecture from the scale of the garden to the scale of the city. This transformation is evident in both Schwartz's practice in particular, and the profession of landscape architecture more broadly over the past two decades. Over that time landscape architects have seen their disciplinary boundaries, professional responsibilities, and practical skills evolve dramatically in favor of urban sites and subjects.

In many ways this commitment to the city is an historic return to the origins of the profession in which the landscape architect was conceived as an urbanist uniquely capable of addressing the intersection of natural health, social welfare, and cultural edification. At the end of the nineteenth century landscape architecture was understood to be a civic art capable of ameliorating the environmental and social conditions of the industrialized city. More so than at any time in the intervening century, contemporary landscape architecture encompasses an extraordinary range of scales, subject matter, and sites attendant to city making. Most recently this has involved a commitment to ecological process as medium and method for describing urban form.

The contemporary practice of landscape architecture as a mode of urbanism ranges from the design of modestly scaled parks and plazas at one scale through regional or national scale planning studies. These practices extend from the interpretation of heritage landscapes or conservation sites to the remediation of sites abandoned in the wake of industrial processes. Taken together these practices might be read as responses to and management of the environmental, social, and economic impacts of ongoing urbanization. The contemporary practices of landscape architecture occupy an astonishingly diverse array of sites and situations ranging from remote hinterlands to formerly dense urban cores. These practices follow the economic geographies of globalization from the abandoned brownfields of the postindustrial economies in the west through the industrializing emergent economies of the east and to the exploding urban settlements of the informal economies of the global south.

The recent work of Martha Schwartz Partners (MSP) does much to embody and exemplify this range of practice, and to argue for the renewed centrality of landscape architecture as a medium of design in the contemporary city. A brief survey of the work included in this publication reveals a set of themes embedded in the contemporary practice of landscape architecture globally, yet specific to Schwartz's ongoing metamorphosis of scale and subject. This work is engaged in the renewal of abandoned city centers, healing sites of resource depletion, invoking community in the context of population shifts, and injecting urbanity into the void of exurban extension.

Over the past two decades landscape architects have been called upon to instigate the renewal of city centers in the wake of urban violence, either in response to the 'fast' violence of armed conflict or the 'slow' violence of economic restructuring. Over this time landscape has reemerged as a medium uniquely equipped to initiate the spatial, economic, and cultural renewal of formerly abandoned urban cores. MSP's project for Exchange Square in Manchester, England (page 44) is exemplary of this line of work, and has contributed to the revivification of a formerly derelict corner of a classic shrinking city. At Exchange Square, Schwartz not only reanimates a formerly abandoned post-industrial urban space evacuated by the fast violence of terror, her work contributes consequentially to the recuperation of the urban plaza as a genre of contemporary landscape architecture in response to the slow violence of economic restructuring globally.

Over the past two decades landscape architects have been called upon to deal with the origins and ends of industrial processes, and been invited to inoculate sites of extraction, production, and deposition. In these contexts landscape has emerged as a medium of design uniquely capable of cleaning the ground, air, and water, while articulating the memory and meaning of the industrial in material, spatial, and cultural terms. MSP's project for the Geraldton Tailings Landscape in rural Canada (page 150) is exemplary of this genre of work. With their work at the Geraldton site, MSP indexes the ecological and social costs of industrial extraction while rendering that history in cultural form. The project reveals the ultimately urban implications of this remote site's history while contributing a remarkable example to the global body of practice of landscape architecture as cultural interpretation through soil remediation.

Over the past two decades landscape architects have been called upon to insulate communities from the social, familial, and interpersonal impacts of migrations associated with economic, technological, and political change. In these contexts landscape has emerged as a medium of design especially able to mitigate many of the human costs of population migrations associated with economic and political restructuring. MSP's project for the Central Park, Monte Laa in Vienna, Austria (page 178) is exemplary of this genre of work. At Monte Laa MSP's work recollects the origins of landscape as a medium of design in which social welfare, environmental health, and cultural form are interconnected. In so doing, the project ennobles what might have been yet another isolated individual housing project with broader ecological and cultural aspirations.

Over the past two decades landscape architects have been called upon to invoke qualities of urbanity in places absent traditional urban form. In these contexts landscape has emerged as a medium of design well suited to the challenges of staging the programmatic density and social propinquity of the city in places seemingly devoid of urban qualities. MSP's project for the Mesa Arts Center in Mesa, Arizona (page 258) is exemplary of this tendency as it invokes a language and literacy of cultural compression through a medium of horizontal extension and ecological connectivity. At the Mesa Arts Center MSP's work reveals the potential for landscape as a medium of design with a unique affinity for the horizontality, automobility, and extreme cultural dilution characteristic of the North American exurban periphery. With this work MSP produces an effective commentary on as well as a remarkable intervention in the American city at the end of the twentieth century.

Taken together, these expansive roles and responsibilities for landscape as a medium of urbanism speak to the reemergence of the landscape architect as the urbanist of our age. The work of MSP does much to exemplify the newfound status and expanding role of the landscape architect. This publication and the work it describes will likely shift the perception of audiences who first came to know Schwartz's work through her pop-art influenced garden designs of a quarter century ago. For those who have come to know Martha Schwartz Partners work through her more recent urban engagements and their effects, this publication will reveal the work of an energetic and imaginative mind at mid-career, grappling with the ecological imperatives and cultural implications of our urban age. For both audiences this publication reveals the scope of practice through which landscape architects are called upon to employ their art as a medium of design for the contemporary city. The impressive body of work collected here does much to consolidate Martha Schwartz's claim to be considered among the most innovative and imaginative landscape architects practicing today.

Charles Waldheim, FAAR, is John E. Irving Professor and Chair of Landscape Architecture at Harvard University's Graduate School of Design.

Martha Schwartz Partners' Central Park Monte Laa,
Vienna, Austria, 2002

Curating Urban Evolution

Emily Waugh

The Changing City
Cities are constantly changing. With the inevitable cycles of prosperity and decline, political succession, ideological shifts, the rise and fall of industry, war, resources, and immigration, urban areas continue to evolve—growing, shrinking, diversifying, sprawling, and densifying in response to forces of change that act upon them.

Major urban change can be sudden and dramatic (the destruction of London during the Second World War or the arrival of more than one million immigrants to Germany's Ruhr Valley during the Industrial Revolution) or steady and gradual (the consistent growth of New York City or the slowly declining birth rates in Western Europe). Sometimes, a steady and gradual change becomes sudden and dramatic when it hits a critical point. We see this today as the centuries-long trend of urban migration has resulted in more than half of the world's population living in cities. These changes, fast or slow, are the result of the natural processes and human interventions that impact the shape and size of cities around the world.

Change moves with the economic cycles of the city. When the economy grows, the city grows. When the economy suffers, the city suffers along with it. Industries and populations flee in search of other opportunities, leaving behind abandoned buildings, toxic industrial sites, and vacant and derelict downtown cores.

Change follows resources. When a new ore-body is uncovered or an oil well struck, floods of people and industries descend on the area, hastily settling lands that are often too isolated or inhospitable for development. When resources are depleted, these communities disappear as quickly as they emerged, leaving unemployment, shrinking populations, and in many cases, severely degraded and devalued landscapes.

Change can be political. As governmental turmoil and civil wars force large populations to seek refuge elsewhere, these displaced populations must relocate to cities around the world, beginning the difficult process of accommodation and integration. In other urban areas, everyday political decisions lead to shifting land-use patterns, changing development frameworks, and new growth policies, each altering the shape and form of the cities around them.

Change can be brutal. Around the world, war and terrorism continue to blast holes through urban fabric, and natural disasters like hurricanes, earthquakes, tsunamis, and volcanic eruptions swiftly level entire cities and regions. These sudden and violent acts can destroy centuries of history and incremental growth, forcing cities to recover and reinvent urban centers from the rubble and destruction.

These changes, from regional to global, are often played out in detail at the neighborhood scale: previously vibrant city centers become vacant with the death of industry; some derelict post-industrial sites and toxic resource-extraction landscapes gentrify while others further decay; some districts become denser and more diverse with surges of immigration while others thin out; and new neighborhoods emerge on the outskirts of cities as urban populations continue to grow.

To successfully navigate this change, cities must adapt, shift, grow, build, re-build, preserve, and renew—providing a solid and flexible base to efficiently guide transition toward a healthy *and* sustainable future.

The Stable and Elastic Urban Landscape

Within these constantly evolving urban conditions, the city's public realm landscapes—streets, parks, and open spaces—carry an intense responsibility as the shared resources of the city and the physical connections that bind it together. They can both catalyze change and absorb it. They can remain constant through cycles of upheaval and they can adapt to new conditions as cities transform around them. To remain sustainable, they must be both stable and elastic, capable of holding the past and catalyzing change for the future. This is no easy task.

The most successful and enduring public spaces are those that have made indelible impacts on the lives of the people who use them, and that have become entrenched in the identity, culture, and daily activity of their cities and neighborhoods. These spaces, like Central Park in New York and Hyde Park in London, offer an ideal paradigm for sustainability, as they remain vital by continuing to evolve along with the increasing complexities and demands of the contemporary city. They perform socially, economically, politically, and environmentally, providing for existing populations while accommodating new and diverse ones, structuring new uses, attracting growth, and sustaining ecological health.

Agents for Change

Parks and open spaces do not only adapt to forces of change, but also have the power to guide, shape, and curate the evolution of cities as the most effective catalysts for urban transformation.

Over short periods of time and for relatively small budgets (compared to building development or major infrastructural works), urban landscapes can dramatically change the character of a neighborhood and provide an immediate emotional, physical, and visual impact on the people who use them—completely transforming the perception of a place, and as a result, transforming the place itself.

These agents for change breathe new life into dying city centers, reclaim toxic resource landscapes, adapt to and accommodate shifting populations, and provide the framework to guide the growth of the city. They can forge an identity for a new development or an old neighborhood in need of regeneration, they can stand as beacons of positive change to a suffering area of a city, they can create a destination within a neighborhood to attract visitors and residents, and they can serve as visible signals of transformation for potential investors and existing residents.

Recycling Space

Contemporary cities are the result of ongoing evolution and change, of natural processes and human interventions built in between and layered on top of one another, constantly evolving into new or altered versions of themselves.

What appears to be an innocuous meadow may be a toxic industrial site, an urban square the roof of a hidden parking garage , and a park may once have been an active quarry. Traffic interchanges, brownfields, vacant lots, streetscapes, industrial waterfronts, derelict parklands, polluted waterways, failed housing developments, and defunct transportation infrastructure provide an opportunity for new life and a new role within the changing city.

Recycling space is not an incidental process, but rather, a deliberate and creative act. It is shaped by a strategic outlook requiring intense understanding of a place and the ability to translate the historic, present, and future needs of the city into a precise and effective landscape design that will become part of its identity and its daily life. Recycling space means guiding the transformation of urban sites, neighborhoods, and cities as they continue to evolve into the future.

In the process of curating urban evolution, the questions become: How cando we breathe new life into urban sites and shape the process of their transformation? What will most effectively translate the benefits of the past into the foundations for a sustainable future? And what will provide the most powerful visual, emotional, and experiential connection to the place for its current and future users?

The Work of Martha Schwartz Partners and the Expanded Field

Martha Schwartz Partners' work catalyzes urban change. Their unmistakable public spaces bring new vitality into neighborhoods through their visual clarity, their emotional impact, and their ability to be absorbed completely into the life and culture of the cities around them.

From defunct mining villages and depleted resource landscapes to dying industrial centers and rapidly expanding urban neighborhoods, Martha

Schwartz Partners' work employs the power of design to transform spaces, neighborhoods, cities, and regions. By providing beacons of hope, visible signals of positive change, an unmistakable sense of place, clear identities, and powerful destinations, their work generates change, attracts new populations, integrates diverse user groups, and creates excitement about urban areas that were previously seen as derelict, dangerous, or negative places.

In their unique approach to urban landscapes, Martha Schwartz Partners uses the transformative power of the visual experience to provide new readings, new relationships, and new purpose to urban sites. They recontextualize existing landscapes and objects to provide a heightened awareness of context, and as a result, a closer relationship to the place. They foster a sense of community and emotional connection to garner stewardship for a public space—if people don't love it, it will not succeed. They break past the boundaries of the typical sustainability checklist to embrace an expanded notion of the term that includes social, economic, *and* environmental sustainability.

These principles have long been the foundation of Martha Schwartz Partners' practice, and in the following pages, we will explore how they impact the transformation of urban spaces, each in a different stage of evolution, each requiring a different solution, and each guiding their neighborhoods and cities toward a sustainable future.

A Map to the Book

Recycling Spaces identifies four critical expressions of urban evolution in cities around the world today: dying city centers, depleted resource landscapes, shifting populations, and non-existent urbanism. The different consequences of, and approaches to, each of these phases of evolution are explored through twelve recent projects of Martha Schwartz Partners, from urban squares and parks, to town master plans, to art installations, to brownfield reclamations. Each demonstrates the transformative role of the designed landscape in curating urban evolution. Through illustrations, photographs, and personal stories from stakeholders, designers, collaborators, neighborhood residents, and Martha Schwartz (in blue text) each of the projects tells a different story about the evolution of a site, a neighborhood, a city, or a region.

A testament to the impact that Martha Schwartz Partners' work has had on the lives of the neighborhoods and cities around them is their substantial presence on photo websites such as Flickr and Google Images. In these venues, they are celebrated as the hosts to an endless range of urban activity and city life. Where possible, we have shown you these projects through the eyes (and cameras) of the many people who use and love these popular urban spaces every day around the world.

01.

Dying City Centers

No longer able to rely on their primary industries for survival, many post-industrial cities lose their vitality, as shrinking populations and depressed economies lead to vacant and derelict downtown cores. These cities need to regenerate, finding new ways to cultivate stable populations, diverse economies, and vibrant urban life.

From left: St. Mary's Churchyard, London, England; Grand Canal Square, Dublin, Ireland; New Village Green, Fryston, England.

Grand Canal Square

Since the late 17th century, the Dublin Docklands area has transformed from river estuary, to agricultural fields, to industrial port, to gasworks, to toxic brownfield, to vibrant urban neighborhood. Grand Canal Square, the centerpiece of the new development, has played a catalytic role in the most recent reshaping of this once-forgotten part of town.

Aerial view looking west toward the River Liffey and Dublin city center.

Dublin is a city of change. Through its more than 1,000-year history, the city has been ruled by the Norse, the Normans, the British, and the Irish.[1] It has been an agricultural city, a shipping city, a manufacturing city, a service city, and a technology city. As the economy shifts, Dublin shifts.

Following the flux of Ireland's tumultuous political and economic history, Dublin has been subject to constant cycles of emigration out of the city followed by floods of people moving back in. The city's population has ebbed and flowed with each cycle of upheaval and growth, plague and opportunity, employment and unemployment, boom and crisis.

From its explosive growth in the late 19th century to the unprecedented outflow during the recessions of the 1950s, from the overcrowded Georgian slums to the overburdened outer suburbs following the 1960s clearing of those slums, from the steady decline through the 20th century to the meteoric rise of the Celtic Tiger period, the cycle continues.[2]

The most recent wave of movement to Dublin came during the Celtic Tiger boom of the mid-1990s, when Ireland transitioned from being one of the poorest countries in Western Europe to having one of the fastest growing economies on the continent. As Dublin's new service economy steadily grew and as tech

High density, poor quality living conditions typical of Dublin's working class neighborhoods. c. 1910.

giants Google, Microsoft, Facebook, Amazon, and Yahoo! began establishing their European headquarters in the area, an intense demand was made on the city's limited housing stock. Housing supplies were too low, rents were too high, and many young families were forced to buy homes in Dublin's less crowded and more affordable suburbs.

The Dublin Docklands Development Authority (DDDA) saw an alternative. With a vision to establish a permanent, sustainable population in downtown Dublin, the DDDA developed a plan to transform the derelict 5-square-kilometer Eastern Docklands district into an extension of the city that would not only be the base for new businesses and cultural programs, but also a vibrant residential hub of 22,000 people, providing an attractive alternative for young families who might otherwise move to the suburbs.

The central core of the Docklands area, formerly the site of an active gasworks and some of the city's worst slums, fell dormant when gas production ceased in the early 1980s, leaving a toxic brownfield badly in need of remediation. To transform the area from a derelict industrial site to a vibrant mixed-use development, the DDDA combined an innovative reclamation strategy with a mandate for high-quality architecture and public realm design. The quality of the new buildings and open spaces—especially Daniel Libeskind's Grand Canal Theatre, and Martha Schwartz's centrally located Grand Canal Square—would signal the rebirth of the district and announce the Docklands as a new destination in the city.

The Square, which would be implemented months, and in some cases, even years before the rest of the development, was charged with shaping the image of the new district, attracting investment to the neighborhood, and generating excitement for the upcoming transformation.

View of the Docklands neighborhood.

"The Docklands area has historically been an important part of Dublin, but it was a really tough place to live. Just look at some of the street names around here—there's Bloodstone Alley, and Misery Hill. Now, we've got about 80,000 people living here and nearly 30,000 jobs. We've got Facebook up the road, we've got Google, who just opened their European headquarters here—it is a totally vibrant sector of the city and it's a great place to live. You have restaurants, you have the theater, you have the river. Businesses are growing and there's a young and energetic population. Even in the midst of the recession, you can't get a table on the square at lunchtime. If you look at what this place was 100 years ago, 20 years ago, or even 5, it's amazing."

— John Doorly, Dublin Docklands Business Forum

Top: Fractured green marble fountain in front of the Grand Canal Theatre. Bottom: Perforated metal seating and native grass planters along Quay wall.

View looking south across the waterfront plaza

GRAND CANAL THEATRE

HOTEL
ENTRANCE
FORBES STREET
CAFE AREA
GREEN CRYSTAL PAVE
LIGHTING BOLLARDS
DROP OFF AREA
MISERY HILL
GRANITE TACTILE PAVING
GRANITE CURB
GRANITE TACTILE PAVING
LIGHTING BOLLARDS
STAIR PAVILION
ENTRANCE
REUSED EXISTING PAVING
STONE BENCHES
GRASS PLANTER
LAWN PLANTER
RED CRYSTAL PAVE
WATER FEATURE
STAINLESS STEEL BANDING
ACCESS ROUTE
GUARD WALL
RAMP
VENT
BOLLARDS
STAIR PAVILION
VEHICULAR ZONE
ALUMINUM BENCHES
ENTRANCE
COMMERCIAL BUILDING
RETRACTABLE BOLLARDS

A New Address in Dublin

The Dublin Docklands needed an identity that would be immediately recognizable and associated with the place. The dramatic Libeskind theater already promised to deliver a clear and powerful aesthetic to the district, so rather than weaken it with a conflicting formal language, MSP extended Libeskind's angular lines down to the ground plane, uniting the building and landscape into one larger public space with a cohesive identity. When the sharp lines of the architecture hit the ground, they become a network of dark gray pathways criss-crossing the square and creating a fragmented pattern across the light gray plaza. The paths connect the buildings within the square, but also reach out into the surrounding streets to pull people into and through the plaza.

Site plan, not to scale.

An Invitation to the Grand Canal

"We knew we had to create a sense of excitement about the place, to build up momentum for the project. You need to get people excited, and hopeful, and curious about what was going on. The square was going to be the first visible sign of the upcoming change in the area, so it had to turn around people's beliefs that something could happen here."

To signal that the theater is open to the world, Schwartz created a sparkling red carpet that crosses through the square and up to the front door of the new theater. The red carpet not only welcomes people to the theater, but to the Docklands themselves, signifying the positive change that was beginning to take place in the area. The other end of the carpet extends out over the canal, inviting Dubliners to reconnect with their waterfront. Despite being a waterfront city, the tidal fluctuations of the river and the high quay walls do not afford many opportunities for people to actually engage with the water. Almost without exception, everyone who walks across the site, whether cutting through on their lunch break or coming to the Docklands for a pre-show

dinner, takes a detour out over the water before continuing on through the square.

In contrast to the dramatic bustle of the red carpet, the green carpet, which cuts the opposite direction across the square, provides visitors with a more relaxed experience of the site. The 15-meter-wide swath is defined by raised concrete planters and gets its color from the native grass and perennial plantings within. The vegetation creates a reminder of the river estuary that once lay beneath the reclaimed land. Bright green perforated metal benches add even more color and provide a place for people to sit down and seek shelter from the wind, a rare opportunity on Dublin's blustery waterfront.

Activity on the red and green carpets.

View down the red carpet toward the Grand Canal Theatre.

ZYR

Color in the Gray City

Dublin is a gray city with streets made of granite, cloudy skies, and winter sunsets as early as 4:10pm. The square provides a source of color and light to the otherwise colorless landscape.

Unable to add the color with vegetation (the parking garage below could not support soil for large trees), MSP added brightness to the northern nights with 7-meter-high red light poles jutting at playful angles out of the surface of the square. The lights are programmed to dance up and down the poles, enhancing the energy of the plaza during bustling theater events and providing additional life to the square during quieter times. The light poles, which serve to break down the scale shift between the buildings and the ground plane, instantly became the most identifiable feature of the square and are now synonymous with Grand Canal. Ask anyone in Dublin how to get to the "square with the red poles" and they will be able to point you to the Docklands.

7-meter-high red poles are reflected in the water at night.

"The initial focus in people's minds was on development and on the buildings, but no matter what the quality of the individual buildings, people's overwhelming sense of place was going to be determined by that public space and the public realm of the wider district, as well.

There's a way in which we navigate the city which is about following certain mental landmarks, so it wasn't as much a physical landmark that was important for Grand Canal, but how it registered in people's consciousness and how it entered into their mental maps of the city. If you want to make it something that people are drawn to, you need to imprint it in people's imaginations, in a way that is fun, that is lively. It had to have an identity in and of itself and had to be of cultural and artistic value.

The plaza was built before the theater, so there was a risk that it would feel incomplete without the building, but Martha's work has such a strong visual sense and coherence, that even when it was in place without any of its intended context, people registered it straightaway. They got it visually. They got that the grasses and the planters were the re-emergence of the mud flats that had been there once before. They got the idea of coast...things that weren't that explicit. People got it very quickly and they loved it. And they still love it. It has become symbolic of this area and of the regeneration of the city.

The perception of the Docklands before Grand Canal Square was that it was full of people in gray suits doing business. Now the square says very clearly: this is somewhere fun to hang out, there's waterfront, there's the theater, there are restaurants, there are bars. This is really part of the city. Huge numbers of people began to move into the area with apartments, galleries, shops... it lit a fire of enthusiasm under the whole place."

— John McLaughlin, former Director of Architecture and Planning, Dublin Docklands Development Authority

24-Hour Urban Activity

The square is further activated by the near-constant flow of people busily shuffling between meetings, lining up for a performance at the theater, or taking the time to just sit and ponder the river. From businessmen and women, to black-tie theater goers, to teens from the surrounding Docklands neighborhood, everyone finds his or her own way of occupying the space and colonizing it temporarily while they are at the square.

Along the water's edge, rows of granite benches offer places for people to eat lunch in the sun or to set down their heavy groceries on the way home from the market. These benches, of all different lengths, become fun stepping stones for the population of children who have begun to move into the neighborhood.

The water fountain, which flows out from the theater end of the square, lends constant movement to the site. Its fractured, multi-level surface encourages people, especially small children, to explore and play.

The square's colorful energy and flexible design have allowed it to be heavily programmed with cultural events, performances, and community gatherings. It has provided the set for television shows, lighting installations, rock concerts, and dance parties, and continues to play its own role in Dublin city life.

The square is activated at all hours by the movement of people, water, and light.

Fortified Against Change

For the first time in 20 years, Dublin is once again losing its population. The Dublin Docklands, however, has maintained a stable population and a level of optimism even within the current recession. Nearly all of the residential units are occupied, new restaurants are opening, and the neighborhood continues to attract business to the area. Through the inevitable cycles of Dublin's fluctuating economy, Grand Canal Square remains as a fixed signal of the vibrancy and optimism of Dublin's newest downtown population.

"Even when the rest of the country has no jobs, we were recruiting for the convention center, for the Grand Canal Theatre, the Aviva Stadium. It makes people feel that it's all happening here at Docklands. It's the one place where it's happening."

— Betty Ashe, St. Andrews Resource Center and former Chair, Dublin Docklands Business Forum

Top: The Hive, interactive sound and light show, 2008.
Bottom: The Spheres perform at the St. Patrick's Day festival, 2009.

"We've learned that what we really need are what we call bumping points: parks for kids to play in, BBQ areas, libraries—places where neighbors and community can come together. Grand Canal Square is absolutely one of those."

— John Doorly, Dublin Docklands Business Forum

Opening night at the Grand Canal Theatre.

GRAND CANAL THEATRE

DAF
66 ENO

Exchange Square

On June 15, 1996, an IRA bomb targeting Manchester's economy and infrastructure blasted a hole through the center of the city. Fortunately, no one was killed and this violent interruption gave Manchester an opportunity to regenerate the underperforming area at the heart of the city.

Bomb damage on Manchester's Cross Street after the June 15th attack.

Aerial view looking toward the Cathedral district.

In the late 19th century, Manchester took its place as a world leader in textile processing and distribution. It remained there until the late 1970s and early 1980s, when a shifting economy and globalized trade saw over 200,000 manufacturing jobs lost[1], sending the city into an economic and social decline that saw much of its population leave for opportunities elsewhere.

Once the epicenter of Manchester's industrial legacy, the city center—in particular the Corn Exchange area—had now become an inhospitable, unwelcoming, and unpopulated part of the city. Abandoned buildings and rotting warehouses lent the city a depressed and derelict image, repelling potential businesses, investors, and residents. By 1991 the city center population was down to 900.[2]

The 1996 blast gave the city an opportunity to correct some of the urban planning decisions that haunted this neighborhood, including the disconnect between the old city and the new; the convergence of major traffic routes at the most perilous intersection of the city; impermeability at the ground level due to large, impenetrable blocks of the 1960s and 1970s; the characteristically dense Victorian fabric with little public space; and a lack of destination or identity for the city.

Historic images of the Corn Exchange area show the fabric of Medieval, Victorian, and contemporary Manchester.

As part of the city's master plan for the new "Millennium Quarter," the Corn Exchange was identified as the heart of Manchester's drive to once again grow a vibrant city center population. The new Exchange Square would be the foundation for a complete transformation of the public space that was to mark Manchester's regeneration and provide a civic infrastructure to undergird the city's ambitious retail and commercial development plans.

Martha Schwartz Partners' strategy for creating a lively urban destination where once there had been "nothing but an ugly intersection" was accomplished with three clear and decisive moves: 1. Stitch the city back together by eliminating topographic boundaries; 2. Install flexible infrastructure to accommodate the changing complexities of urban life; and 3. Create a clear link between the history, present, and future of Manchester through highlighting local geology, material choices, furniture, and urban elements.

Crowds at Exchange Square and surrounding streets highlight the success of Manchester's new Millennium Quarter.

"Before the square was here, it felt like the last person who left the city at the end of the working day, turned the lights out."

— Euan Kellie, Author of *Rebuilding Manchester*

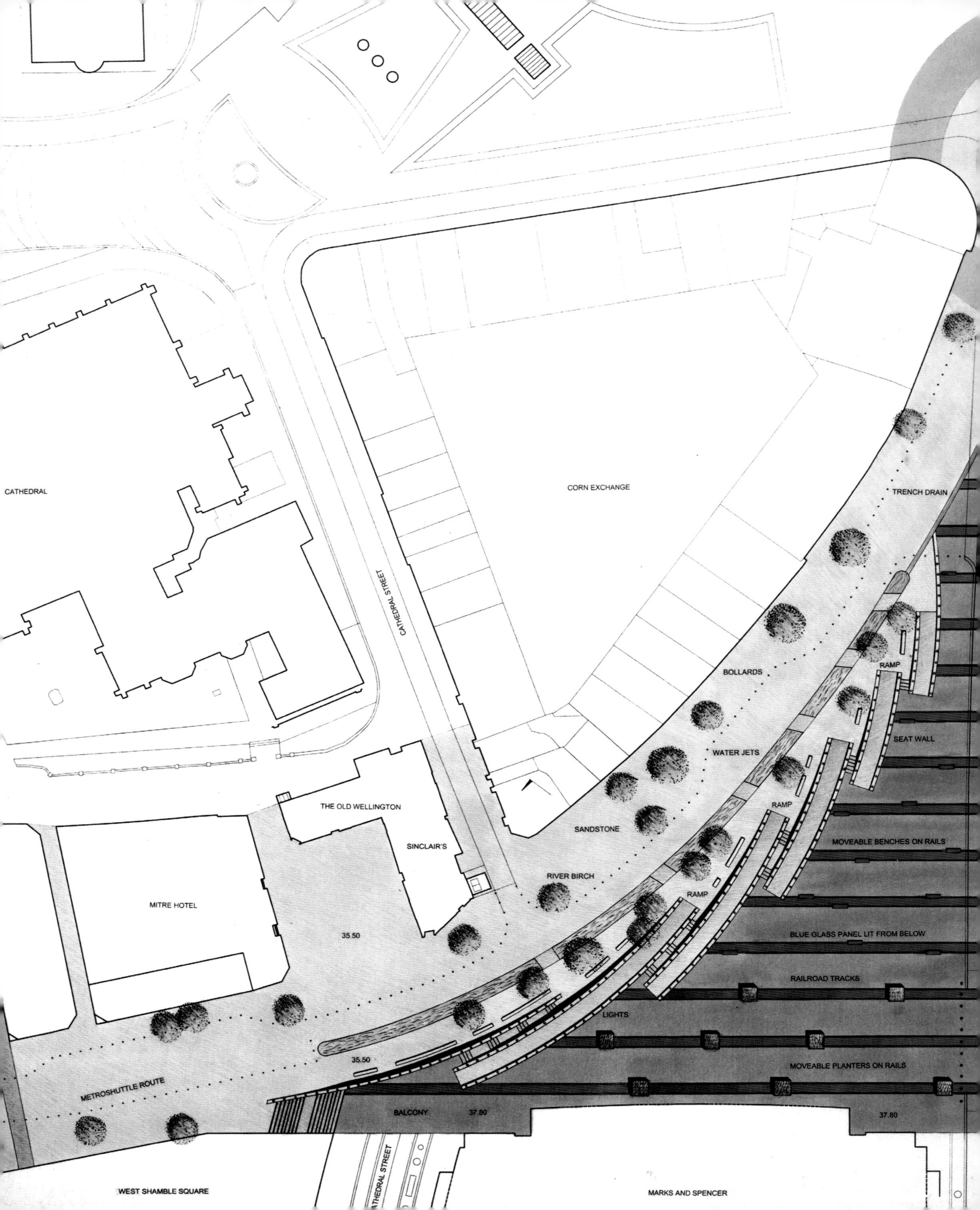

CATHEDRAL
CORN EXCHANGE
CATHEDRAL STREET
TRENCH DRAIN
BOLLARDS
RAMP
SEAT WALL
WATER JETS
RAMP
THE OLD WELLINGTON
SANDSTONE
MOVEABLE BENCHES ON RAILS
SINCLAIR'S
RIVER BIRCH
RAMP
MITRE HOTEL
35.50
BLUE GLASS PANEL LIT FROM BELOW
RAILROAD TRACKS
LIGHTS
35.50
MOVEABLE PLANTERS ON RAILS
METROSHUTTLE ROUTE
BALCONY
37.80
37.80
WEST SHAMBLE SQUARE
CATHEDRAL STREET
MARKS AND SPENCER

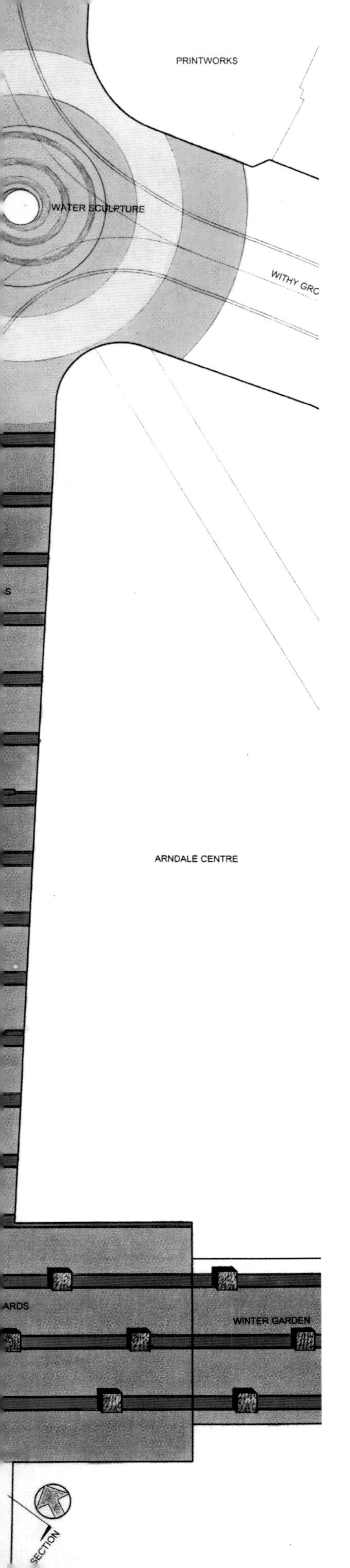

Stitching the City

The Corn Exchange sits at the junction of Medieval, Victorian, and 21st century Manchester, so the first priority was to reconnect (or connect for the first time) the Cathedral district to the north with the expanding business district to the south, by trying to negotiate the 3-meter grade change between the upper and lower portions of the site.

MSP connected the upper and lower territories of the site with a generous sweep of large, gentle ramps that smoothed out the topography, allowing pedestrians to easily travel from the Marks and Spencer Plaza down to the Triangle (formerly the Corn Exchange) or to simply pass through the square on their way through the city. Instead of being an impassable tangle of traffic and large buildings, Exchange Square was now completely connected to the city on all sides.

Site plan, not to scale.

Civic Infrastructure

The ramps are joined together by 1-meter-wide Yorkstone benches that create an amphitheater-style lounge, providing endless seating possibilities for the ebb and flow of the busy square—"You can sit on either side, lie down, hang out by yourself or in a large group… move with the sun as it moves throughout the day… you can do whatever you want on them."

The benches have become part of the city's infrastructure and reflect the constant motion and change of the city throughout the day. At 7am, there might be a solitary reader taking in the morning paper; by 10am he will have been joined by dozens of shoppers and nearby workers passing by to have a coffee or to check out the sports scores on a large BBC screen mounted on the side of the Corn Exchange building. By noon the benches will have disappeared underneath the crowd of people eating lunch, watching the soaps, or taking a break from a morning of shopping.

Sweeping arcs of Yorkstone benches create a large outdoor living room.

"Martha's design was very modern, but blended with the old. It was clear that she had taken very strong readings from the history of the area, and the design took those threads from the history of that part of the city and built them into something modern."

— Sir Richard Leese, Leader of Manchester City Council

"If you go back 30 years in Manchester, we were becoming a bit of a rust-bucket city. We were an industrial city, but the old industry had gone. What future did we have? As a city, we had to re-invent ourselves and how the city-center contributed commercially to the life of the city. We knew that if we wanted a high value added economy—if we wanted people to come into our city center—then we needed to have an appearance to the city center that made it attractive to come into, a place that people wanted to be.

We talked a lot about the recent homogenization of city centers and high streets and we knew we couldn't be just another city center. We wanted things that when you were there, you knew you were in Manchester, that you weren't anywhere else. Even though it is not a big city center, there are different parts that have their own particular characteristics and we wanted to make sure that those characteristics were maintained as we went through renewal activities.

Exchange Square helps us join different neighborhoods with different characteristics. Unlike any other space in the city there is a real connection between 21st century Manchester, 19th century and Medieval Manchester—they all meet at that particular junction allowing connections for people that were not possible before the design of the square. Cities are about people.

Prior to 1996, this was the most dangerous street crossing in the city center, now it is the busiest retail section of the city. The new Exchange Square is something that is very distinctly about Manchester, I've never seen anything like it anywhere else. The whole area is transformed."

— Sir Richard Leese, Leader of Manchester City Council

Regional Geology

Not only is Exchange Square at the junction of old and new Manchester, it also sits on the junction of two geological formations—a huge nose of Yorkstone at the Cathedral side of the square and an adjacent bed of granite underneath the new shopping center. MSP's scheme for the square further highlights the relationship between the above- and below-ground conditions of the site. "The structure of the space is the structure of the underlying geology. We knew that in order for this space to resonate with people, it had to reflect the local context and history, it had to be of this place."

MSP also resurrected the figure of the ancient fortifications ditch that carried a stream between the Irk and Irwell rivers until it was condemned as a sanitary open sewer and culverted in 1600. The sweeping arc of the "Hanging Ditch" marks the boundary of the two rock formations. The Hanging Ditch fountain, constructed from purple basalt columns, follows the course of the Hanging Ditch and is one of the most recognizable and beloved features of the site. At all hours of the day, you can find children playing stepping stones, couples strolling hand in hand, or passersby reaching down to touch the water—anyone walking through the space cannot help but walk on it. It has become integrated into Manchester culture, supporting thousands of anxious England fans during the 2006 World Cup and acting as a regular participant in local festivals and civic gatherings.

The 'Hanging Ditch' fountain reveals the site's geological structure.

TRIANGLE
LEISURE BARS
OFFICES

Industrial Legacy

The cultural significance of the Corn Exchange and Manchester's industrial history strongly define the character of the city and its population. "The history of Manchester is such a vivid one. The Industrial Revolution, which is such an important piece of modern history, happened here. It was important to recognize that legacy in the design for the square." The city, formerly known as "Cottonopolis," grew to its peak not only because of the success of its textile production, but also due to its advanced transportation legacy.

In recognition of Manchester's railway history, the upper plaza of the square features a series of "flatbed" benches made from unused railway parts and real train wheels sitting on "tracks." These smaller seating surfaces offer a low-key alternative to the larger stone benches on the lower plaza.

The industrial history of Manchester is reflected in the modern materials and forms of the upper plaza. Stainless steel and granite are presented here in rigid mechanical lines, in contrast to the curved, smooth Yorkstone of the lower portion.

"I think a successful space is where there is something to be experienced by people at many different levels. If people are looking for meaning, they will find it, but what is most important is that people enjoy it, and they are proud of it, and want to use it, and that they come to use it so often that it becomes part of who they are as citizens of the city."

Flatbed railroad benches remind visitors of Manchester's rich industrial past.

LAKERS

The Heart of the New City

As a testament to Manchester's resilience to the difficulties of its past, Exchange Square immediately became the center of Manchester's new life and the image of its restored civic pride. At all hours of the day and night, the now more than 11,000[3] city center residents and others from all over Manchester flock to the square to shop, eat, watch TV, and to be a part of the buzzing urban atmosphere. By activating an immediate and accessible destination for Manchester, Exchange Square catalyzed the transformation of the city center from an inhospitable dead-zone to the commercial and cultural heart of the city.

The square has become the center of civic life and activity in Manchester.

"I remember my first trip back into the city after the bomb; it was very eerie, very strange. There were buildings with the windows smashed; it was in tatters, behind hoarding…to see this in your own city was really disturbing, but it gave us a chance to start over.

Before the blast, you wouldn't go to the Corn Exchange because you didn't particularly want to. The whole area was dismal, it was a very non-descript part of the city, it was an area that just sort of existed, it didn't have any character, there was no activity, there was no vibrancy. Corporation Street, where the bomb truck was planted, was five lanes of traffic; crossing the road to get to the Corn Exchange was perilous. There was a little bit of open space there, but it wasn't a place you would choose to go to relax. It didn't have a destination, it was poorly linked to the rest of the city, and most people didn't know it existed.

The area is different now because there is activity at all times during the day. There are millions of people who use that space a year, millions. You see people stopping there, sit down, take stock of things, watch the big screen on the side of the triangle. It's a destination; if you say to anybody in the city, Exchange Square, people know it.

We all make choices about where we want to live. I have chosen to live in Manchester because I love it here, I love what the city offers. I am a product of what the city is trying to accomplish. I came here to go to university and I stayed here. I live here and I work here. You can have as many apartments as you can build in a city center, but if people don't have a reason to live there, they won't live there."

— Euan Kellie, Author of *Rebuilding Manchester*

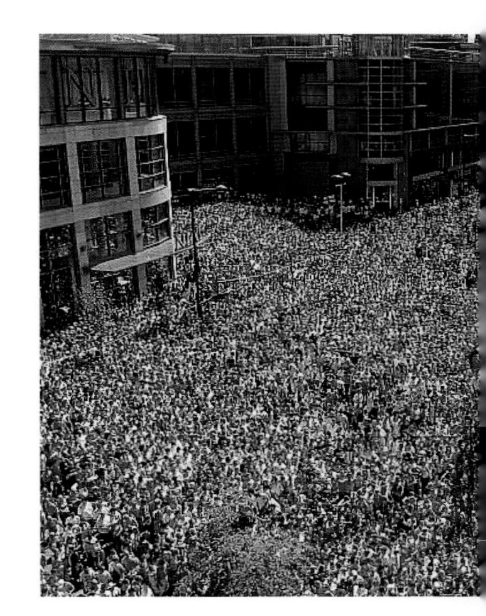

Left: Manchester Street Choir Festival.
Right: England vs Paraguay, FIFA World Cup, 2006.

St. Mary's Churchyard

The Elephant and Castle was once a thriving hub nicknamed the "Piccadilly of South London."[1] Since a brutal post-war modernist rebuilding effort dehumanized its public realm, the area has gained a reputation for being a dirty, traffic-dominated, and dangerous part of the city. That same public realm has once again become the agent for change in this vital London neighborhood.

View of children's play area looking toward the Elephant and Castle Shopping Center.

Elephant and Castle (known by locals as "The Elephant") sits just across the river from Central London and was once a thriving urban hub known for its department stores, music halls, and theaters. After being leveled by German air raids and subsequent fires during the Second World War, the area was remodeled with a typical post-war, brutal, car-centric, modernist plan dominated by traffic infrastructure, massive concrete housing blocks, and inhospitable ground-plane conditions.

Top: Aerial view of one of Elephant and Castle's two large traffic roundabouts
Bottom: The Heygate Housing Estate, pre-demolition, 2009.

The post-war plan rebuilt the neighborhood around a new road network and two six-lane traffic circles with no pedestrian crossings at street level. Pedestrians are instead forced into the network of dingy subway underpasses that have come to characterize the dark and dangerous reputation of Elephant and Castle.

As part of the same rebuilding effort, the pre-war Victorian and Edwardian housing stock was replaced with several massive modern housing blocks, including the Heygate Housing Estate, which upon its completion in 1973, was one of the largest (and some argue, most depressing) housing estates in London. The giant, windowless Elephant and Castle Shopping Center, which was meant to revolutionize retail when it was built in 1965, has been repeatedly voted London's ugliest structure.

Over the five decades since, the dense and active area has gained a reputation for being a dangerous, dark, and dirty corner of the city, and has often been the scene of TV crime dramas (such as Law and Order) and gangster movies including Harry Brown, starring Elephant and Castle native Michael Caine.

In order to reverse the negative perception of the area and to transform the Elephant and Castle into a safe and desirable area of London, the city would have to overturn the brutal infrastructural planning of the post-war period and rediscover the more human-scale experience of this dense urban neighborhood.

"Southwark is about 60% social housing and most of that is flats, so most people in the area don't have their own gardens or access to outdoor spaces, so parks and open spaces are extremely important to the people here."

— Rebecca Towers, Manager, Southwark Council Parks and Open Spaces

Inhospitable pedestrian conditions at street level.

"The poor quality of the public realm at the Elephant and Castle is one of the main things that holds the area back from reaching its full potential.

First, we needed an improved public realm to overcome the negative perception of the Elephant as not a very safe place, not a very clean place, and not a very pleasant place to spend time. Fear of crime is as important as actual crime levels, so we needed to change that perception in order to get investment into the place and to release its full potential.

Secondly, if you improve public realm, you encourage development. It's hugely important when developers try to sell homes that they can show people that the place is safe, that there are places to spend time and enjoy yourself, that there is a sense of community. We are promoting a dense urban environment, so we need spaces that can cater to the additional people who are going to come into the area.

We needed to implement an early project to demonstrate how we could take a space that exists at the moment and transform it into a town center that attracts a lot of people to use it. St. Mary's Churchyard showed us that it was possible because it had not been very well used prior to the intervention, but has now become such a vital part of the neighborhood. Before Martha took the wall down, people couldn't see into the space, so no one was using it except for a few street drinkers and vagrants. Now, by providing access to it and providing more facilities, you get much more use out of it. It is fantastic."

— John Abbott, former Director, Elephant and Castle Regeneration

The iconic symbol of the Elephant and Castle.

In 2004 Southwark Council approved a development framework to regenerate the Elephant and Castle. The comprehensive plan would convert the southern roundabout to a regular junction, restore pedestrian movement to street level, and tear down the Heygate Estate, offering over 5,000 new and replacement homes in its place. The scheme also includes an integrated public transport hub, new civic buildings, almost one million square feet of retail, and five new parks and open spaces.

The district of Southwark recognized that the key to galvanizing community, making a livable neighborhood, and successfully transforming the Elephant and Castle was to conceive an integrated public realm for the whole area that was of a high quality commensurate with the goals of the regeneration. The public realm would be the foundation for the entire development and would set the standard of quality for the new urban fabric.

Martha Schwartz Partners was brought in to oversee the public realm plan for the 60-hectare development zone and to ensure that the streetscapes, parks, and open spaces proposed by the architects were adequate to support a healthy and vital population in the area.

"Unless you involve someone early on to think about how developments will impact the street level experience, open spaces tend to be the dribs and drabs that are left over after FARs, traffic patterns, and building heights are settled. It was an enlightened move for Southwark Council to recognize the impact of a good public realm from the outset, and one that will make the difference to the success of the regeneration efforts."

But before the city could begin any of the major infrastructural redevelopments necessary to transform the neighborhood, they needed an immediate and highly visible beacon to attract investment, to catalyze momentum for the project, and to demonstrate to a weary population that the council was committed to reversing the ills that had plagued the neighborhood for the previous five decades.

The site for this pilot public realm improvement was St. Mary's Churchyard, a historic open space adjacent to the southern roundabout. This was already a busy transit hub and soon to be a pedestrian-heavy urban node. No stranger to evolution, the churchyard had already been through multiple changes and had not actually had a church on it since 1876, when St. Mary's Parish was moved to nearby Kennington Park Roard, so that the yard could remain as an open space for the benefit of the steadily growing city.

The churchyard featured an open lawn shaded by mature London Plane trees, but was failing as an urban space because it was isolated from the surrounding neighborhood by an imposing wall and dense vegetation. The space was seen, as much of the Elephant was, as a dangerous and unpleasant place to spend time.

Martha Schwartz Partners designed a scheme that could re-integrate the park into the Elephant and Castle, while still providing some relief from its fast-paced, dense urban context.

St. Mary's Churchyard, before.

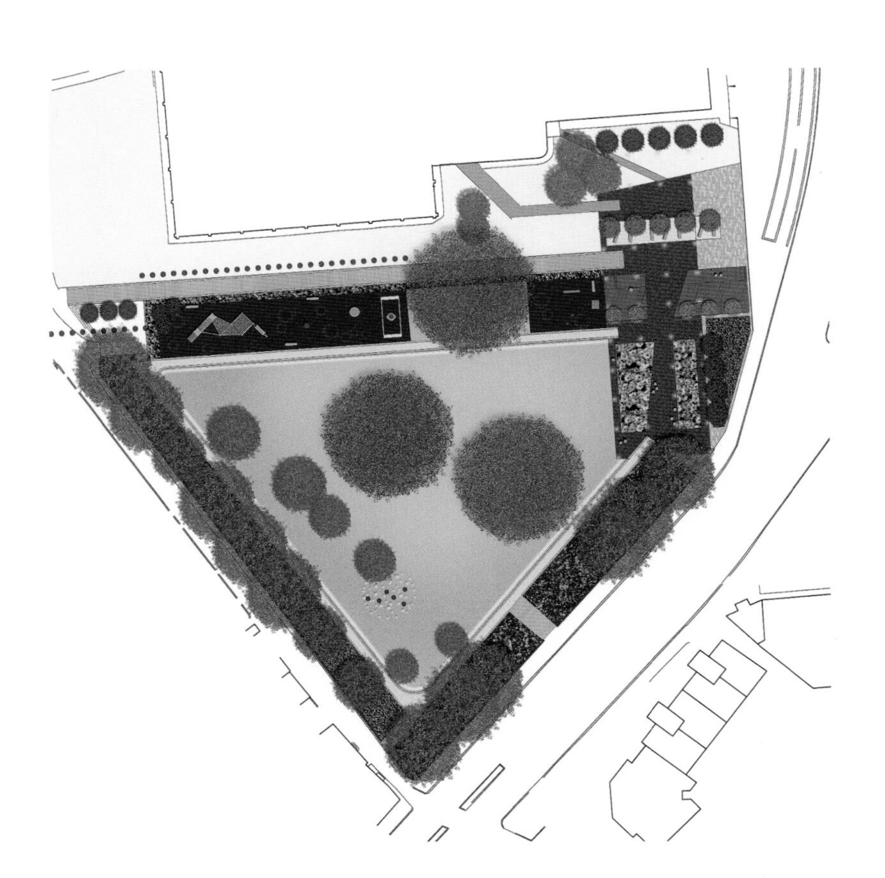

Open up to the Neighborhood

"The site was sitting alone and a little bit sad and a little bit scary, so the first thing we did was tear down the imposing brick and wrought-iron wall and densely vegetated mounds that cut off the site from the surrounding neighborhood."

In addition to integrating the site into its context, tearing down the heavy perimeter wall also opened up cross connections and sight lines, which immediately made it a safer, more active, and more inviting space.

Most importantly, it sent a message to the residents of Elephant and Castle that they were active participants in the transformation of their neighborhood and that they were invited to enjoy the positive change that was happening.

After the park edge had been opened up to the neighborhood, it would need a buffer from the intensity of the intersection to the east and a transitional edge that

would signal that St. Mary's Churchyard is a place of respite from the constant hustle and bustle of the Elephant. The designers created this threshold with a walkway that frames the perimeter of the space. The walkway protects the quiet lawn on the inside, while remaining open to the neighborhood on the outside. It invites people to explore the edge of the space or travel directly through the yard from the west to the east.

Site plan and aerial views showing relationship to the surrounding neighborhood.

"High-quality open space makes you feel like you are in a place that is important and that is cared for; it means you are valued if you have access to that."

— Rebecca Towers, Manager, Southwark Council Parks and Open Spaces

The perimeter walkway frames the inner park area, shielding it from the busy transit hub.

Emerica.

Doorstep to the Elephant and Castle

At the east side of the churchyard, the walkway opens up into a plaza that creates a doorstep to the neighborhood, providing a threshold between the churchyard and the intense nexus of cars, buses, trains, and pedestrians that flow through the busy transit hub. The plaza is a civic gathering point with rows of benches inviting commuters to take a break while they wait for their buses or trains to take them across the river to work or to bring them home again at the end of the day. Playful striped orange and white versions of London's typical crosswalk "Belisha Beacons" indicate that this area is a crossway between the busy transit hub and the tranquil churchyard. By taking these iconic pieces of London infrastructure out of their usual context, the designers let people know that they are still in London, but that this place has its own distinct identity. This area also features a slightly raised wooden platform, or stage, that welcomes any spontaneous urban activity—such as a neighborhood gathering, a skateboarding, or an impromptu musical performance.

Plaza area with cross walk beacons provides a waiting area for transit users and a gateway to the residential neighborhood beyond.

PISTON
CUP
95

Spine of Activity

The east entrance doorstep marks one end of a central spine of activity that connects the transit hub at the east with the residences to the west. This spine provides a convenient and welcoming passage for pedestrians coming and going between their homes and the transit hub and shopping center. This slice through the park also contains the children's play area, which is designed to serve a variety of ages, and in particular the younger children who need a safe place to play. The popular playground features bright pink and orange rubber mounds and play equipment that add a strong visual identity to the yard—a shock of color to the otherwise hard, gray transit landscape.

Celebrate the Existing Character

The expansive lawn is the largest area of the park, and remains the most similar to the original churchyard. The bumpy grass surface and huge mature trees provided the space with a unique character that the designers simply enhanced to reinforce the identity of the park and the neighborhood. Because the churchyard was formerly a burial ground, the designers, unable to dig, worked with the original ground condition, adding even more lumps and bumps to enhance the already dynamic surface. The bumps were created by inserting large black-and-white cast concrete spheres into the lawn surface. The spheres sit in a circle around a large weeping willow, framing the beautiful tree and welcoming visitors to come and sit in its shade. These simple insertions help to break up the larger grass area into smaller spaces, providing places for playing, picnicking, or just hanging out.

Large concrete spheres are embedded in the lawn to enhance the existing character of the park's surface.

Changing Perceptions for a Changing Future

The post-war planning mistakes and subsequent regeneration efforts at the Elephant and Castle illustrate the power of the public realm to influence people's perceptions of a neighborhood and, in turn, the reality of that neighborhood. St. Mary's Churchyard is working hard within the regeneration effort to overturn the negative image of the Elephant and Castle. It is a popular, highly used space and continues to serve as a bright and vibrant indicator of the positive changes to come. Residents already feel the momentum of the regeneration and, slowly, perceptions of the Elephant and Castle are beginning to change as it is once again seen as a vibrant urban hub.

Fryston Village Green

Once a thriving mining community, the West Yorkshire village of Fryston had only 76 houses remaining after the closure of the mine in 1986. With no industry, no services, and diminished hope, this small tight-knit community would need a powerful symbol for change to help them grow toward a sustainable future.

Football on the vacant Fryston Green, 1987.

AIREDALE
AIREDALE

The tiny village of Fryston is less than 20 kilometers from the center of Leeds, the second largest financial service center in the United Kingdom. But with only 76 homes, no gas and sewage service, and just one dead-end road leading into and out of the village, Fryston feels more than a century away from its neighboring city.

Like hundreds of other towns and villages in the North of England, Fryston was established to support a coal mining operation (or colliery, as they are called in the United Kingdom). After the first coal was drawn from Fryston Pit in 1874, the town grew into a vibrant, hardworking community of 500 households. Separated by railway tracks from the rest of Castleford, Fryston was a completely self-contained village with its own school, church, pub, and shops.

The nationalization of the coal mines in 1947 combined with decreased productivity in the colliery set off a 40-year slide for the village, which would see some of the older terraced houses being demolished as early as the 1950s. The nation-wide miners' strike of 1984 marked the final decline of the once-famous Fryston pit. As the men were out on the picket lines with nearly 150,000 other miners across the country, a fire broke out in the Fryston mine that blocked half the pit, rendering it unprofitable after the strike.

Shoveling coal at Fryston Pit.

By early 1986 the mine was officially closed. Almost overnight, headgear was torn down, winding towers were dismantled, and pits were sealed, leaving what former Pit Deputy David Wilders described as a "ghost pit." Not long after, houses, chapels, and shops were quickly demolished as men and their families moved to newer homes 25 kilometers away in Selby, where a new mine had opened up, offering new opportunities for survival. For the older generation who stayed behind, life in Fryston was a difficult daily reminder of the earlier booming days of the proud mining community.

By the time English Partnerships began exploring ideas to reclaim the mining lands and revive the dying village, all that remained were two aging rows of terraced housing, crumbling, poorly drained roads, decaying sidewalks, and an overgrown vacant field with rusty play equipment in one corner. This was their Village Green. Fryston needed new hope, new civic infrastructure, and new life if it was going to sustain itself into the future.

English Partnerships brought in Martha Schwartz Partners to develop a master plan that would help to restore Fryston to a vibrant community with the population and resources it needed to once again function as a healthy and self-sustaining village. The regeneration plan for the 5-hectare area surrounding the village would add 150 new homes, improved civic infrastructure, and a new Village Green, providing the foundation for a new population and a new civic pride. The remaining 93 hectares of surrounding mining lands would be restored to a country park with 8 km of bicycle trails and bridle paths, 40,000 new trees, and a new green edge along the Aire River, which flows just behind the village.

From left: Residents look on as the last of the coal mining operation is demolished. Fryston, England, 1986; Masterplan prepared by Martha Schwartz Partners to accommodate new houses, amenities, and the new Village Green.

Martha Schwartz Partners' master plan envisioned a cohesive community along a connective spine that was anchored by a pub and a community center. The spine–a pedestrian and bridle route–would become the village's main thoroughfare and would provide the frame for the heart of the expanded community, the new Village Green.

"A lot of the turn-of-the-century terrace houses have been demolished across the Wakefield district as people have left them for newer properties. The area has not been seen as a nice place to stay and live, but we wanted to turn that around. We wanted to build on what we've got and keep the people together who've lived there for many years. But we also wanted to add to that, to build their capacity and maybe get a shop in there again, a market, and some services."

— Andy Golding, Wakefield Council

The Village Green was the first element of the master plan to be built. In this role, it would signal a new image for Fryston to attract a future population, and offer hope and commitment to the current community for whom change from the outside had not always been positive. "It was not easy at first to engage the people of Fryston in the process. They had already been through so much with the aggressive mine closures, and they had heard so many broken promises before. The prevailing attitude was, 'This is one more thing that is probably never going to happen.'"

The new Village Green would need to engage the community. It would need to be firmly rooted in

the traditions of Fryston's past, while at the same time moving the village forward into the 21st century. The designers approached this challenge with three guiding principles derived from observing the village and working closely with Fryston's residents: 1. Extend existing activities into the park; 2. Reconnect the Village Green with Fryston's rich mining heritage; and 3. Set the stage for the future population.

Site plan, not to scale.

Extending Fryston Culture into the Green

The front steps of Fryston's terraced houses have always been the primary public space of the village. Every morning, people sit out on their stoops to drink their tea, to catch up with their neighbors, and to watch their children play. The stairs are the threshold between people's private lives and the community. To fully connect the new Green into this existing model of village life, MSP's first design move extends the front steps of the terraces out into the park. A series of smooth concrete benches stack up to connect the park to street grade and are essentially a series of front steps, inviting people to come out of their homes and into the new community. The old, crumbling front steps and inadequate sidewalks are replaced with new ones to match the material of the benches, extending the threshold of people's homes down the steps, across the street, and into the park.

Horse riding is also a strong tradition in Fryston, and for some it is a way of life. If the Village Green was going to serve the people of Fryston, it would have to serve their horses, as well. Horse riding is integrated into the park with a sand bridle path that runs the length of the Green at the street edge, keeping horses and riders a safe distance from the road. A set of cast-iron bollards, designed by Antony Gormley, marks the edge of the trail where it crosses with the pedestrian pathways into the park.

Left page, top: Working and socializing on the front steps.
Bottom: A series of stone benches extend Fryston's front steps into the green.

Coal Mining Legacy

The new Village Green points Fryston toward a hopeful future, but also looks back into its proud and industrious past. The village was built on the tradition of coal mining and of making a livelihood by engaging with the materials of the earth. The Village Green celebrates this rich mining tradition with a powerful, manmade aesthetic appropriate to the rugged, hard-working community.

The mining process is made visible in the park as the surface of the site is broken by a deep gauge out of the earth that reveals what looks like a coal seam underneath. This black, rubberized surface forms the base of the new children's play area, whose gently sloping seat walls provide places

for older children to hang out, ride their bikes, and get some privacy from their watchful parents on the front steps.

At the west end of the green, one important mining artifact remains from the original playground—a red colliery wheel that stands as an eternal monument to the town's mining heritage and the legacy of Fryston Pit. No matter what the future holds for Fryston, the colliery and its mining legacy will always be present in the community.

A slice through the groundplane reveals a black rubber play surface reminiscent of a coal seam. The edges of the seam become stepped seating.

"I remember the village when I was a child just after the Second World War, when it was a rather big colliery churning out coal for generations. It was a thriving village, but it was cut off from the rest of Castleford, so it became a very close-knit community and quite a proud community in that they contributed to the industrial benefits of the rest of the country.

When the coal mines were shut down quite brutally in the 1980s, most of the village was demolished. So what you came across was a much demoralized community—diminished and destroyed, really. As a community, we were crying out for regeneration. Fryston needed this perhaps more than anywhere else. What we needed immediately was to improve the look of the village and the esteem of the local people. They had to be convinced that something was going to happen to improve their environment and the derelict land. That input would have to be significant, and doing something at the center of the village, at the center of their lives, really, was most important.

Since the green has been done, the fact that the residents were proud of the center of their village made them better able to cope with the fact that for three years, developers have been churning up the land around them, cleaning it up, dragging cars out of the basin where the coal barges used to be. The fact that they could have something immediately that they could be proud of while all this work was going on around their village...they knew that good things were going to happen because that had already happened with the square."

— Alison Drake, former Fryston resident and Chairman, Castleford Heritage Trust

Foundation for the Future

As Fryston prepares to absorb a new population, the Green offers a safe and welcoming environment for the young families who will be joining the community. The playground and recreation area invite endless opportunities for play, and an informal outdoor theater is ready for public performances and community gatherings. The cairn, a form created from stacked rocks, rises from the center of the stage to provide a signifier of growth and change. The spiral mound of cut stone gradually tapers to a series of glass bricks that are lit to provide a beacon for Fryston, day and night. In addition, a new lighting scheme extends the hours of the park and creates a safe environment after sunset, which in winter can be as early as 3:45pm at this northern latitude.

The Cairn provides a strong symbol for the village as it moves forward into the future.

A Part of the Community

As Fryston continues to evolve, the Village Green is slowly being welcomed as a member of the community and is well used by residents and local children. As construction crews and bulldozers literally move the ground around them, and the prospect of a new population becomes more real, the residents of Fryston have the Village Green, *their* Village Green, as a constant reminder that this upheaval and change will yield positive results. "The idea that a landscape could make people happy with a giant change is a lot to expect," but as the people of Fryston find new ways to make the space their own, it will become part of the tradition of the place and provide the foundation for a vital and sustainable future for the village.

02.

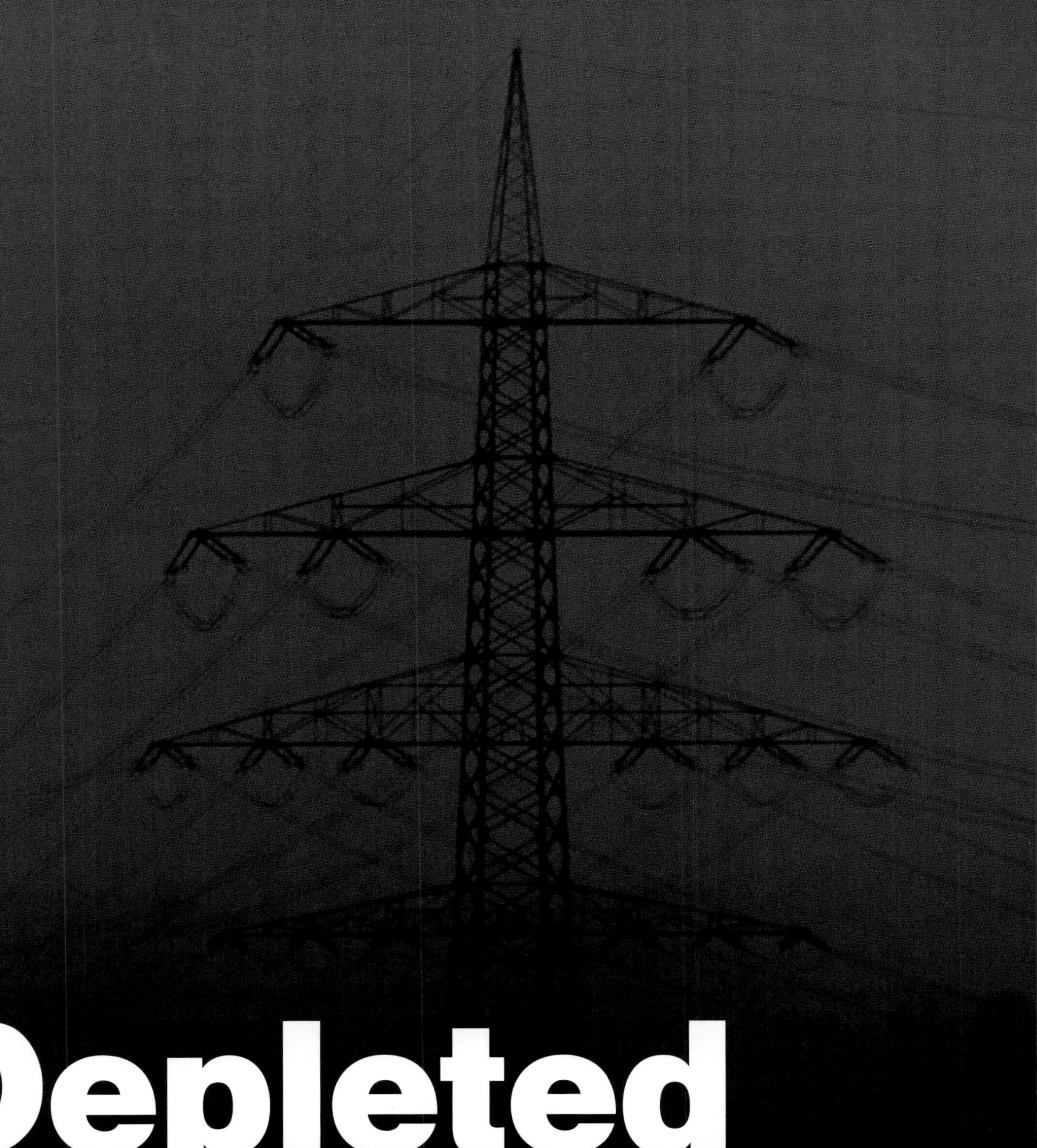

Depleted Resources

Resource extraction sites are paradoxically the world's most and least valued landscapes. Once the last ounce of gold, coal, oil, or gas is extracted, the perceived value of the land disappears with the last of the resource, leaving scarred, toxic landscapes and devastated economies. Populations are forced to either move away or live in the ruins of the past. These towns, villages, and cities need reinvention: new life, new purpose, and new identity.

From left: Power Lines, Gelsenkirchen, Germany; Winslow Farms Conservancy, Winslow, USA; Geraldton Tailings Landscape, Geraldton, Canada.

Winslow Farms Conservancy

Hank McNeil was looking for a place to train his field trial Labrador Retrievers. What he found was an abandoned clay quarry and a lifelong commitment to conserving a rare and precious piece of open space in the New Jersey Pinelands.

Aerial view of Winslow Farms.

Hank McNeil's search for a country property led him just 22 miles southeast of his downtown Philadelphia home to one of the many abandoned clay quarries scattered throughout southern New Jersey.

The pit, which had originally been quarried to provide clay for the bricks to construct neighboring Philadelphia, had been abandoned in the 1950s, leaving behind an unreclaimed wasteland of compacted clay soils and piles of sludge remaining from the brick-firing process. The rest of the 600-acre site, formerly active farmland, was also abandoned and left to natural succession.

As the site was slowly colonized by a new community of pines and scrub oaks, southern New Jersey was quickly being taken over by a different population. The sprawl from Philadelphia, which had traditionally spread westward into Pennsylvania, had changed its course and was heading east across the Delaware River toward the relatively inexpensive land in New Jersey. Quickly, huge swaths of New Jersey's unique (and now nationally protected) Pinelands were consumed by tract housing, strip malls, and parking lots.

During this real estate boom, the land that would later become the Winslow Farms Conservancy had provisionally been sold to develop 700 houses with plans to simply fence off the quarry, which had been deemed impossible to reclaim. Several years after that deal dissolved, McNeil saw an opportunity to coalesce his engagement with dog training with his love of art and

Clay quarry, before.

design, and purchased the property. McNeil envisioned a country retreat where he could train his dogs and where he could lay the foundation for his artist's retreat, a vast outdoor art park where artists like Sol Lewitt could come and work on site-specific pieces in the landscape.

With each subsequent phase of the project, McNeil entered further into what would become an innovative reclamation effort to transform the abandoned clay quarry and dense forest into a productive certified organic farm and open space conservancy. But first, the entire property would have to be reshaped and the hard, inhospitable clay soil completely reconstituted if it would ever be able to support plant life.

Due to the size of the property and complexity of the proposed transformation, McNeil brought in Martha Schwartz Partners to help him formalize a vision for the site. With the master plan, Schwartz provided a strategy to organize the diverse and seemingly conflicting land uses

that would need to simultaneously operate at Winslow Farms. Schwartz worked with these non-traditional adjacencies to heighten awareness of the land and to apply an experiential and cultural layer to the working landscape. The result was a hybrid reclamation strategy that would transform the previously devalued site into a cultural, recreational, and productive resource.

Schwartz and McNeil approached the reconstruction of the site with four principal moves: 1. Reclaim the clay quarry to reintroduce plant and wildlife communities to the site; 2. Devise a selective "clearing plan" to delineate separate spaces for separate functions; 3. Define functional and experiential connections through the site via roads and visual corridors; and 4. Insert unfamiliar elements to provide a new reading of the landscape.

Clay quarry, before.

"The site hadn't been occupied since the 1950s, so all hell had broken loose. The crime situation was really bad: People had been murdered in the quarry, there was a motorcycle gang—bad things happened. I'd go over on Sundays and it was terrifying; we received threats. A dirt bike racing team used it for their practices, and the rest of the site was basically a dump. We uncovered about 50 cars, two dump trucks, thousands of tires, millions of broken beer bottles, beer cans, people's refrigerators...It was an unattractive scene.

Not everyone was happy to have us here at first. We would put up no trespassing signs and come back to find bullet holes in them. A lot of people in the township were suspicious of what we were doing; there was even a rumor that we were in partnership with Disney and that we were going to turn the property into a theme park. But once people saw what we were trying to do, they started to get enthusiastic. It was a slow process, but we started to see results. The first time I saw an osprey over the quarry, it was great, and now there are swans back in the lake and we have hundreds of wild turkeys and quail. The criminal activity is gone, the national field competitions we have here every year fill up the motels and restaurants in the area, and we have now preserved over 600 acres of open space that would have otherwise been developed into a subdivision. It is an incredibly fulfilling project because people said it couldn't be done."

— Hank McNeil, Owner, Winslow Farms Conservancy

Reconstitute the Quarry

The ecological ambitions of the project worked alongside the cultural to recreate the plant and animal habitat that had long been absent from the site. Within Schwartz's master plan, ecologist David Smart helped to reclaim the quarry portion of the property, isolating and capping the sludge from the firing activities, re-grading the surface for proper drainage, and bringing the hard, inhospitable clay soils to life to support new, productive vegetative communities.

The reclamation process was both innovative and economical. The trees that were removed in the land clearing process were chipped on site, mixed in with the ground-up clay soil, and fertilized to create an organic layer that was then redistributed across the entire quarry as topsoil. This new organic layer could sustain a new planting of hot-weather grass species that were carefully selected on three criteria: seed heads to attract wildlife to the property; a maximum height of 12 inches so they wouldn't require maintenance; and tolerance to survive in the highly acidic woodchips and hostile clay. To prevent the entire new layer of soil from washing down the quarry's steep slopes in the first rainstorm, it was stabilized with a spray of clover that would hold it in place until the grasses had established their roots.

"I think the project only worked because I didn't know that you couldn't really do the things we ended up doing. Everyone we consulted said, 'No, it's not possible,' but I was like an excited kid and I kept asking, 'What if? What if we tried this? What if we did that?' I had no idea what I was getting into."

— Hank McNeil, Owner, Winslow Farms Conservancy

Wood chips help aerate the inhospitable clay soils and provide an organic medium for planting.

Selective Clearing Plan

The entire property outside of the barren clay quarry was covered with dense pine and oak forest. The aim of the clearing plan was to carve identifiable spaces out of the forest that could support the variety of uses proposed for the site. The property would first be a country retreat for McNeil to train his dogs and host national field trial events. Secondly, it would function as an art park where artists could come to work. And thirdly, it would need to be restored to its previous function as a working farm, where McNeil would grow certified organic Saltmeadow Cordgrass, Echinacea, and Beachgrass.

Schwartz conceived of the property as a great park and choreographed a series of spaces or "rooms," each connected but capable of supporting its individual function. Schwartz carved the great rooms by clearing strategic swaths of trees out of the dense forest, whereby the forest edge formed the walls and the corridors between the rooms. One room contained the quarry; others, agricultural fields; and others still, experiential rooms for exploring the character of the landscape.

Large rooms are carved out of the densely wooded site.

With Martha's leadership, we created a paradigm that can be, and probably should be, copied. There are over 239,000 acres of clay, sand, and gravel quarries in New Jersey alone: imagine the potential if other people would try to do this. With some ingenuity and good bartering skills, it can be done.

— Hank McNeil, Owner, Winslow Farms Conservancy

Connections and Continuity

At 600 acres, the property required clear visual and physical connections for orientation and movement through the site. The large outdoor rooms are connected by long corridors that slice through the forest in perfectly straight lines. These corridors are designed so that even at long distances, someone traveling through the property is able to see down the length of the entire passage and into the next room. The glimpse is enough to entice visitors to continue walking, and in doing so, they are able to piece together a complete picture of the property as a whole. With this in mind, Schwartz carefully choreographed a sequence that would help orient visitors to their location within the larger site. Over multiple explorations through the property, visitors would gain a full understanding of its particular features and adjacencies.

Schwartz created a further visual link through the site with a consistent planting of evenly spaced rows of cedar trees distributed across the entire property. Because it is an amalgam of several different pieces of land purchased over many years, the character and narrative of the landscapes were disconnected. The trees create a distinct yet familiar connection to both agricultural and cultural landscapes, and worked to provide continuity between the disparate site elements. When you emerge from the woods to see a perfectly clipped row of cedar trees in the middle of a farmer's field, there is no question that you are at Winslow Farms.

Large corridors provide visual and physical links across the 600-acre site.

Contrast to Provide Heightened Awareness

"Hank understood the value of art and design to re-characterize a degraded site through both an environmental change, but also a change in perception. We created value out of something that people thought was nothing."

The tree grid combined with other obvious manmade insertions into the natural landscape add a cultural overlay to the property, clearly highlighting that this site is the result of a century of human intervention.

The trees, which seem oddly out of place in their perfect rows, make legible the evolutionary nature of a cultural landscape and suggest that these agricultural fields might once more be in transition toward a new use. In one area of the property, the grid is stretched to a distance of 93 yards to illustrate the footprints of the suburban housing lots that were scheduled for the site before McNeil purchased it.

As part of the clearing plan, positive forms were designed to be left after the negative voids had been cleared for the large rooms. When the designers had finished with the subtraction, huge circular and oblong clusters of trees stand out in the center of fields to sharpen the point for visitors that this was not quite a forest and not quite an agricultural landscape either.

Repeated forms and unexpected adjacencies provide a heightened awareness of surroundings.

"Prior to the 1970s, there was no land use law in New Jersey; there was nothing in place for zoning, so people just kind of went willy-nilly. When the Pinelands Commission was established, we set up designated growth areas to protect the remaining open space from the sprawl that New Jersey has been experiencing for many years. We didn't want to take away the value of the last piece of earth that New Jersey has and cover it with sprawl.

The Winslow Farms site was originally slated for development, but now it is something for us to hang our hats on here in Winslow. The more land that can be put into permanent land preservation is a good thing for New Jersey; we are so overpopulated already and the whole state needs to change its image. All people think about when they think about Jersey is the Sopranos and Bruce Springsteen and the factories and the ports. But it is different here. This is special."

— Ed McGlinchey, Winslow Township Public Works Director and Commissioner, New Jersey Pinelands Commission

Rows of evergreens are used throughout the site to provide a sense of connection across the vast property.

Innovation to Create Value

In addition to providing a retreat for McNeil and his family, the Winslow Farms Conservancy has recast the image of the previously derelict land and has provided a source of pride and value for the Hammonton, New Jersey area.

The success of the project comes from the optimism of the team and the innovative processes of negotiation and exchange that allowed them to transform the site with a small ecological impact and an even smaller budget. The woodchips for the soil reclamation were harvested and chipped on site; roads were constructed from ground-up concrete from a major New Jersey highway improvement project; mulch would come from the county's fall leaf dumps; remains from the clay furnaces, old refrigerators and stoves, and tires from the abandoned quarry form the base of a berm that provides a topographical feature from which to view the site; and the wood for Schwartz's running

fence that marks the boundary of the site was obtained free of charge from a telephone company that was discarding hundreds of old poles.

The careful reclamation of this piece of land has preserved 600 acres of what would have otherwise become suburban sprawl and has restored it to a productive landscape with active vegetative and wildlife communities that no one could have imagined emerging from an abandoned quarry full of rusty trucks… except for maybe Hank McNeil and Martha Schwartz.

Power Lines

For more than a hundred years, Germany's Ruhr region was the industrial heart of Europe. By 1989 it was one of the most environmentally devastated regions in the world and the center of an art and design led renewal curated by the International Building Exhibition (IBA).

Overview of installation site showing planting patterns and hallway.

During the Industrial Revolution, Germany's Ruhr region was transformed from an agricultural landscape to an industrial powerhouse. The region, known for its rich deposits of high-quality coking coal, quickly became the industrial heart of Europe, with over 300 coal mines in operation by 1850.

This rapid growth fueled a massive demand for labor in the area's mines and attendant iron and steel works. This attracted over 500,000 migrants from the former eastern territories of Germany and nearly two million more from across the rest of Europe, causing a population increase of more than 500 percent in the second half of the 19th century alone.[1]

Industry in the region continued to thrive until the 1940s, when, as the primary manufacturing force behind the German troops in the Second World War, the Ruhr became a strategic target for allied forces' attacks, forcing an estimated one-third of the mines to close.[2] High oil prices and the steel crisis of the early 1970s, along with the restructuring of the steel industry in the early 1980s, made German coal uncompetitive on the world market. Combined with steadily dwindling coal deposits, this signaled the end for the former industrial giant. By 1984 the region recorded its lowest population numbers since 1939.[3]

Industrial infrastructure at the Zollverein Coalmine Industrial Complex.

What remained was a scarred, toxic landscape characterized by derelict industrial complexes, polluted waterways (which had served as the region's industrial sewers), compromised soils, tailings ponds, and massive slag heaps from coking operations.

The region required a complete ecological, economic, and cultural renewal. The government, determined to stem the steady outflow from the region, launched an unprecedented program to overturn the degraded and hazardous image of the area. The International Building Exhibition (IBA) Emscher Park was launched in 1989 to reinvent the image of the Ruhr region through new cultural uses and innovative reclamation programs. Contrary to what its name suggests, the IBA is not exclusively about buildings, but a complete approach to redeveloping the built landscapes of the region for the future while maintaining a view to its industrial past.

IBA made a ten-year investment for 120 projects across the Emscher Park region that would generate the ecological, cultural, and economic transformation of the former industrial wasteland, using artists and designers to recast it as a healthy and valuable cultural resource. The 800-square-kilometer region along the Emscher River Valley would be reconceived as a "green belt" and exhibit park connecting the 17 towns along the river through regenerated brownfields, reclaimed forests, and existing recreational areas. Following IBA's Change Without Growth policy, each of the projects within the scheme would incorporate existing industrial structures and build only on previously developed land instead of spreading out new construction into the surrounding greenfields.

The projects ranged from large-scale and permanent (like Latz and Partner's 200-hectare Duisburg Nord Park, and OMA's Zollverein coal complex regeneration), to temporary art installations (like Christo's Gasometer piece), each designed to ascribe a new use for and new reading of the region.

In 1999, IBA invited Martha Schwartz to install a temporary exhibition on the only hill in the region (the rest are all slag heaps). The site was a farmer's field outside the former coal city of Gelsenkirchen. IBA issued only two guidelines: 1. Everything Schwartz built had to be done sustainably; and 2. The project had to pay for itself with the crops harvested from the installation site.

Using only standard farming methods to create the installation, Schwartz and her husband Markus Jatsch (Jatsch Laux Architects) worked closely with farm operator, Mr. Stricker. According to the artists' planting and plowing plan, Stricker would plant, reap, and bale all of the construction materials for the project and would plow the patterns of the installation into the hillside.

From left: Duisburg-Nord Landscape Park; View overlooking Ruhr Valley's transportation corridors and industrialized horizon.

Cultural Influences Shaping the Land

In the spirit of IBA, whose goal is to recharacterize the Ruhr region through art and design, Schwartz and Jatsch would offer a new reading of this particular landscape by creating a scene that was both familiar and fresh, resulting in a heightened awareness of the factors that shaped the land. The installation was completely constructed out of typical agricultural crops and processes, but this was clearly not a regular farmer's field.

Schwartz and Jatsch recast the site through the lens of the different forces that shaped its physical and cultural existence: the massive power lines that sliced through the landscape, the agricultural and industrial influences on the land, and the statue of Otto von Bismarck that stood brutishly in a knot of locust trees at the top of the hill. The idea was to heighten the visitor's awareness of the power relationships behind even the most benign agricultural landscapes.

A statue of Otto von Bismarck and a hydro corridor represent two different sources of 'power' on the site.

Intersection of Power

A small pathway had been worn into the hill by years of visitors crossing up and down the field to see the statue of Bismarck, the so-called "Iron" Chancellor, who first unified the separate states of Germany into a powerful empire. The point where the path intersects with the power lines overhead was identified as the "Point of Power" and the epicenter of the visitor experience. Using bales of hay that had been grown for this purpose earlier in the season, the designers constructed a 30-meter-diameter circular room. The hay was baled in industry-standard black plastic wrap and stacked to create the room's 2-meter-high walls. Where the walls meet the ground, a coal floor describes the region's industrial past and lends a thought-provoking darkness to the "black heart" of this landscape.

Another harvest of hay bales, these ones in red plastic wrap (the color of power), was used to construct an extremely narrow hallway that ran between the black heart and the Bismarck statue at the top of the hill.

All visitors that came to the site would want to run through the hallway to the top of the hill to see the view, but would find themselves in a power play as they negotiated who would go first up the narrow hallway. Only one person could lead, and everyone else had to follow. Once at the top of the hill, visitors would finally be able to take in the whole hillside and again be confronted with a familiar scene that was suddenly unfamiliar.

Typical bales of plastic-wrapped hay are used to construct a room and a hallway that accentuate the intersection of power.

Rooms on the Hillside

Corn and clover, common sights on a farmer's field, are used here as structural elements to segment the site into different sections. The crops, planted by Stricker in typical straight agricultural lines, are angled to create an effect that is anything but typical, further heightening the tension between the visitors' expectations of an agricultural field and the influence of the surrounding landscape.

Parallel rows of corn pulse outward from the power lines, taking their angle from the sharp run of the clusters of wires that slice efficiently across the rural landscape. Running almost perpendicular to the corn are alternating strips of hard, bare earth and strips of soft, inviting clover. As the corn grew over the summer season, the space was rapidly transformed as different "rooms" crept up the hillside toward the statue. No longer a farmer's field, the site became a French Baroque garden of rooms, with each room offering a slightly different view or experience of the site. People would lie down on the clover floor, play hide and seek in the corn, or have picnics on the hillside, all the while trying to get their bearings in this agricultural landscape that had been curiously twisted into a garden.

At the end of the summer, it would all be ploughed under and a new planting cycle would begin.

Corn and clover are used to 'grow' different rooms across the landscape and up the slope of the farmer's field.

A New Identity for a Healthy Future

The Ruhr Valley and IBA offer an example of the agency of art and design in reshaping the identity and character of an entire region. Before IBA, the Ruhr was known as the black lung of Europe. Now, it has become a rich cultural landscape that offers a sustainable future for the region by repurposing the relics of its industrial past. The very infrastructure responsible for its degradation has become the building blocks of its resurrection, illustrating that simply making the decision to try to see something differently can catalyze a cycle of transformation that allows that thing to actually become quite different.

Aerial view of installation showing its relationship to the surrounding landscape.

Geraldton Tailings Landscape

After the last of Geraldton's gold mines closed in 1970, the town was left with no economy, a steadily decreasing population, and 14 million tons of tailings as a reminder of the industry that had once sustained the town. Could Geraldton's worst feature be reshaped to become its most valuable asset?

Terraces under construction with Lake Kenogamisis beyond.

With 75 percent of Canada's population living within 160 kilometers of the United States border, most of the towns dotted across the northern reaches of the country's ten provinces were established on forestry, mineral speculation, and mining. When ore veins are depleted or operations become uneconomical, mines are forced to close, leaving many of these resource-reliant communities with high unemployment, boarded-up shops, and diminished populations as people leave in search of other opportunities.

The town of Geraldton is clustered with hundreds of other mining communities in the sparse, mineral-rich landscape of the Canadian Shield, a nearly impenetrable igneous shelf that covers almost half the country. Like many of the towns in this area, Geraldton sprang up from the harsh rocky landscape as a mining camp during the Sturgeon River Gold Rush of the 1930s.[1] The town, a station stop along the Canadian National Railway line, continued to grow into a vibrant community bolstered by the area's thirteen operating gold mines.[2]

Top: Historic view of the Macleod-Cockshutt mine. Bottom: Driving along the Trans-Canada Highway near Geraldton.

The mines in the region continued to boom for another 35 years, but when diminishing ore veins and low gold prices through the 1960s made the intensive Canadian Shield mining process no longer viable, they began to shut down one by one. When the last remaining operation, the Macleod-Cockshutt mine, ceased production in September 1970, Geraldton was left with no economy and 14 million tons of toxic tailings as a reminder of the industry that had once sustained the town.

Following the mine closures, many towns in the region have turned to tourism in an effort to attract some of the 100,000 annual travelers passing by on the northern extension of the Trans-Canada Highway.[3] The highway cuts through many of the nation's small communities as it makes its way across the entire country, but due to Geraldton's low-lying topography and more than 50 percent surface water, engineers were forced to build the highway 4 kilometers south of town, leaving it invisible to passing motorists. What drivers would see instead was a three-story-high pile of toxic-looking tailings that stretched for 1.5 kilometers along the side of the highway, giving an impression not of a small community, but an abandoned wasteland. Geraldton was not only unable to attract passing motorists, it was actually repelling them.

The headframe of the Macleod-Cockshutt mine still stands at the turnoff toward Geraldton.

When Barrick Gold inherited the Macleod Mine as part of a larger purchase in 1994 they were met with the challenge of reclaiming a site that had been abandoned for over 25 years and reviving a town that had been shrinking for just as long.

Barrick began with conventional remediation and closure practices including stabilizing the suspected contaminating source of the town's drinking water, securing the mine shafts, removing the buildings and mining infrastructure, and planting grasses and tree seedlings to re-vegetate the stripped and barren landscape.

One critical question remained: What to do with the massive piles of waste rock that had been hastily deposited by the side of the road, leaving Geraldton with little hope of attracting visitors and boosting its struggling economy?

In this case, conventional methods would not be enough.

The mine tailings are transformed into a roadside attraction.

"When we took over the Macleod-Cockshutt mine, it had been sitting there, unreclaimed for 25 years. It was a source of contamination and an eyesore that was causing big problems for the town. The ministry of transportation had received complaints that on windy days, debris from the tailings pile was sand-blasting the traffic and causing visibility problems. There was a drainage ditch between the tailings and the highway with ugly orange-brown water in it. It was fairly sterile, but it looked like the worst possible contamination, and it was right there for everyone to see as they passed by on the highway. That was the calling card for Geraldton. You would be driving through forests and over lakes, then you would come into this clearing and on one side is the Macleod mine headframe, and on the other is a kilometer and a half of these yellow tailings, and an old junkyard right at the turn-off for the town. People probably slowed down because they wondered what the tailings were, but once they registered what was going on they would speed up to get beyond it."

— John McDonough, former Vice President of Environment, Barrick Gold

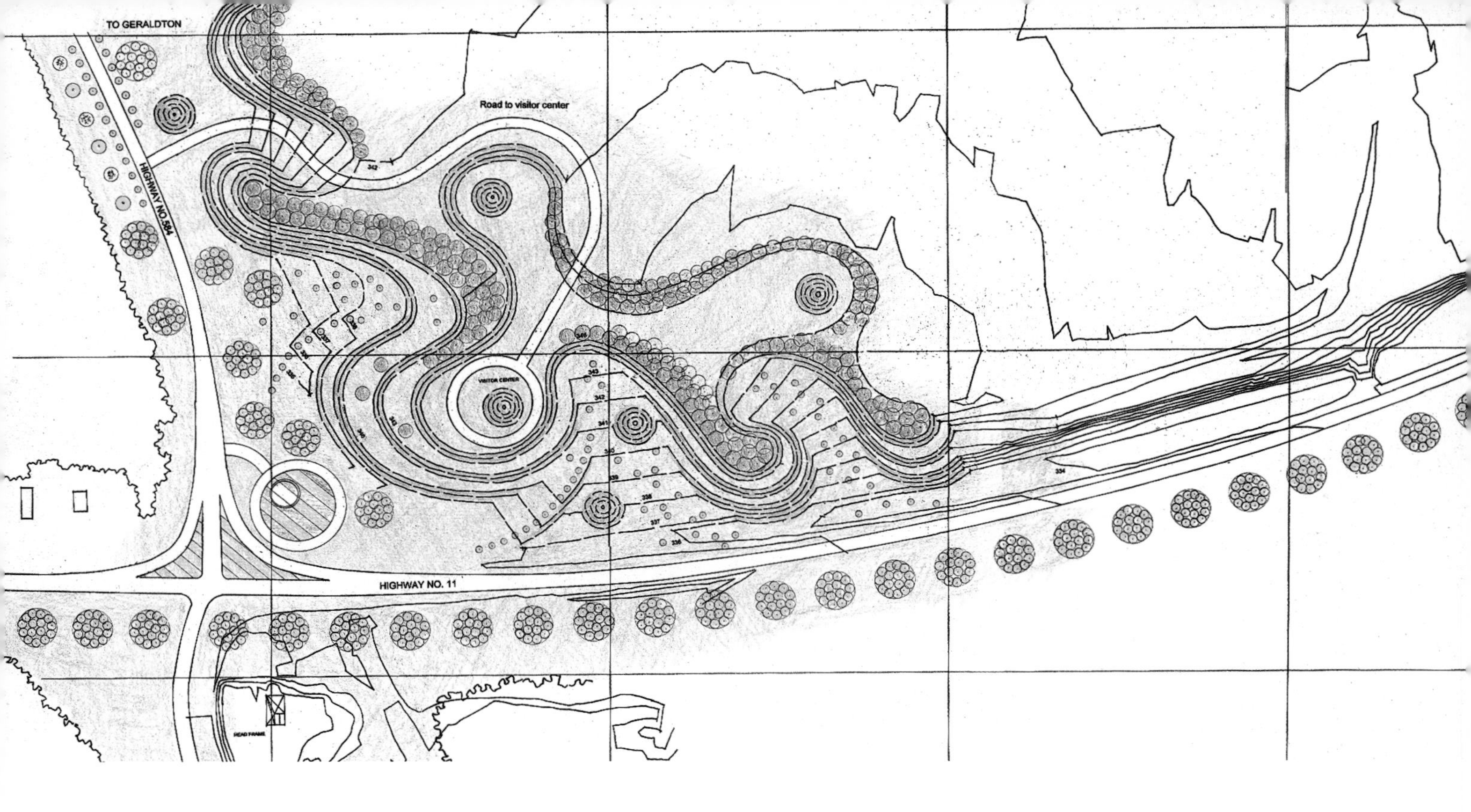

A New Approach

Typically, mine tailings are left in place and stabilized through re-grading and vegetation, but following standard procedure was not a sufficient solution for John McDonough, the then-Vice President of Environment for Barrick Gold. After working one year earlier with Martha Schwartz and her students from the Graduate School of Design at Harvard on a similar project for the Ortiz mine in Santa Fe, New Mexico, it was clear to McDonough that ecological restoration was only half the story: “The real project would be sustaining the town’s economy by finding a way to get people to slow down on the highway and make a stop in Geraldton. Martha opened our eyes to think maybe there could be a way to use these mining byproducts as a way to change people’s perception of the terrain, from dirty mining waste to something of interest.”

Schwartz then led another Harvard studio, this time exploring ideas for how to reshape the tailings of the Macleod mine to create an attraction that would raise people’s curiosity and entice them to pull off the highway and into the town. “The challenge we gave to the students

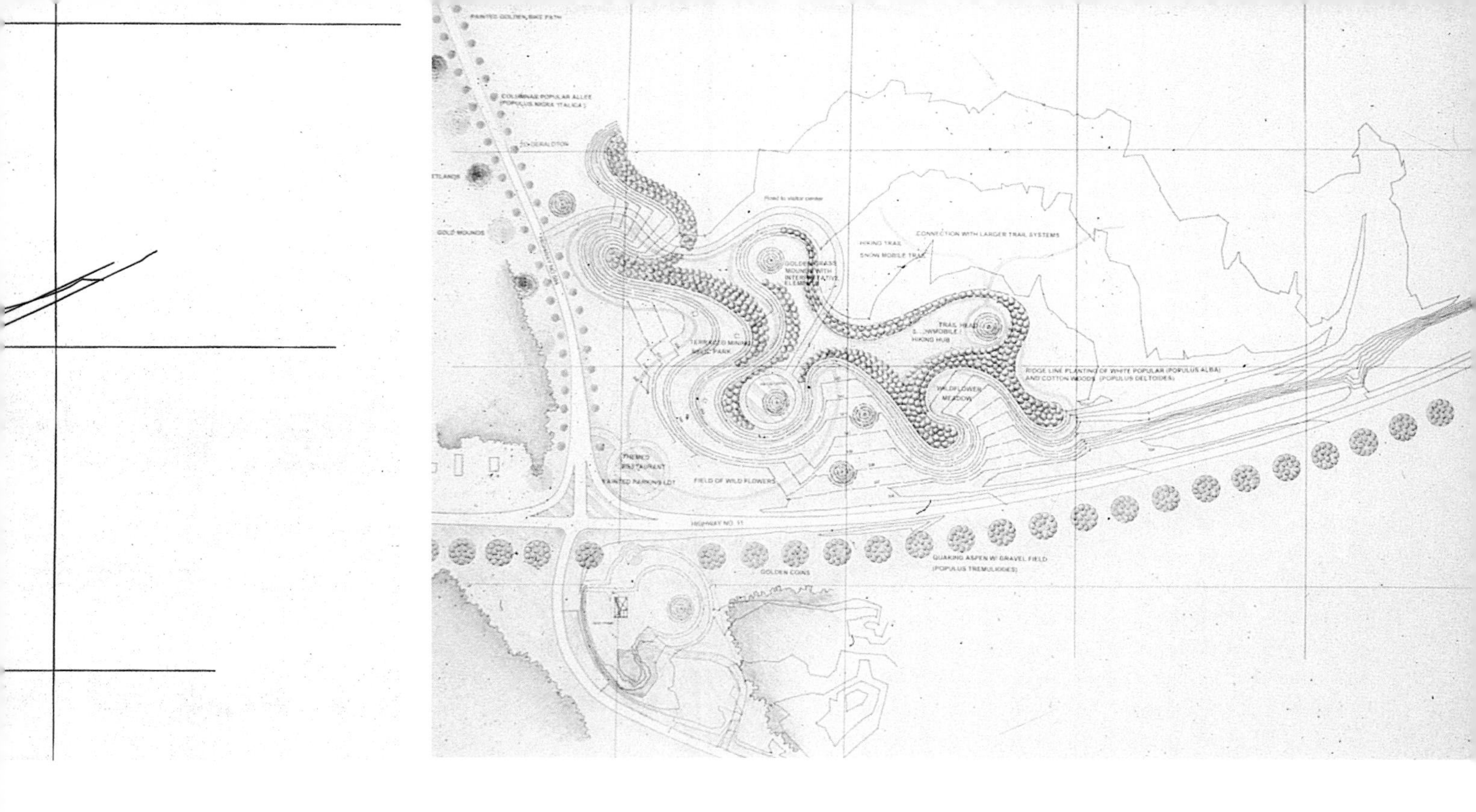

was: How can we transform these tailings into a landscape that was beautiful enough, and striking enough that it would register in people's minds along this long and naturally beautiful stretch of highway?" The students teamed up with local engineering students to create designs that were innovative and exciting, but also practical and structurally resolved. At the end of the term, the students presented their designs to McDonough and the Barrick team, further opening their eyes to the latent potential of this currently devalued landscape.

Barrick later approached Martha Schwartz Partners to develop a plan for reshaping the tailings into an attraction for the town of Geraldton that would provide a new image for the community and a new source for their economy.

Left: Site plan, not to scale. Right: Planting plan, not to scale.

Curiosity on the Roadside

As the Trans-Canada Highway snakes its way across 7,821 kilometers of the Canadian landscape, it slowly unveils a picture of the country as you have never seen it. Through tidal flats and glacial lakes, through peat bogs and boreal forest, every part of the country is identified by its local landscape and remembered for its particular topography and vegetation. To make a place for Geraldton in this powerful national narrative, MSP would have to construct something so visible and so memorable that it would entice people to get out of their cars to take a picture and hopefully retain their curiosity for long enough to stay for a snack, a meal, or even overnight.

The approach toward Geraldton in either direction is characterized by a low-lying spruce- and birch-dominated landscape with little topographic range. In contrast to this condition, Schwartz and her team created an exaggerated

topography that abruptly announced that something here was different. A giant curvilinear landform and a series of smaller cone-shaped piles are sited directly at the turn-off to Geraldton, creating a topographic gateway to the town that lies just 4 kilometers down the road.

Panorama showing the relationship of the landform to the edges of the Trans-Canada highway (right) and the road toward Geraldton (left).

Gold Mining Heritage

"We knew we couldn't return the site to its 'natural state,' first because it had already been altered so significantly, and second, because as soon as it blends into the surrounding landscape, it loses its ability to be distinct. Instead, we had to make something that would stand out just enough from its context that it would stir curiosity in passing drivers. If that curiosity was strong enough, they would pull over to find out what was going on."

The landform borrows its structure and shape from the engineering techniques used in pit mining, and builds to its nearly seven-story height in a progression of "benched" terraces. The 5-meter high terraces recall the mining legacy that has defined so many communities in Canada's north, but are, as Schwartz describes them, "A little too graceful

to be a product of an actual mining process." This alone is enough to entice many drivers off the highway and up the hill to the new Geraldton Interpretive Center that is perched atop one of the curvilinear landforms. Lee Macodrum of the Geraldton Interpretive Center said, "Most people pull over just to find out what these things are. The fact that it is such a unique shape, it makes people slow down and say, 'What is that?'"

The landforms are planted with a golden palette of native grasses and shrubs that add rare color to the gray-brown landscape and remind visitors of Geraldton's mining past.

From left: The toxic-looking tailings landscape before; The tailings re-shaped; The tailings planted with golden native wildflowers to attract attention while stabilizing the soils.

Using a heritage grant secured by the town, the remaining tailings were used to construct a network of nature trails and to add nine more holes to the Kenogamisis golf course, which was originally designed in 1938 for mine owner Fred MacLeod by legendary Canadian golf course designer Stanley Thompson. Both the nature trails and the golf course continue to be popular attractions for visitors to the area and a source of pride for the people of Geraldton. "Nearly everyone brings their out-of-town guests here and they all comment on the landscape. They are just so surprised to see something like this in Northern Ontario." (Lee Macodrum, Geraldton Interpretive Center)

Aerial view of the Trans-Canada Highway, the Geraldton Interpretive Center atop the tailings landform, and the Kenogamisis golf course.

Reshaping the Image of a Town (Literally)

This iconic topographical landscape has become the identifying feature on that stretch of highway, and the defining image of the town of Geraldton. Passing motorists, most of whom have never heard of Geraldton before, find themselves compelled to pull off the road and up the hill to the Interpretive Center to find out more about where they are and what they are seeing. Once out of their cars, many of these people—who are from all over Canada, the United States, and Europe—stretch their legs on the heritage trails before heading into town for a meal or to stay overnight.

Through Barrick Gold and Martha Schwartz Partners' innovative approach, Geraldton's worst feature has literally been reshaped into its greatest asset. This has permanently altered John McDonough's approach to the reclamation process and provides a clear message about the power of design to alter the perception of a landscape, a town, or an entire region.

The terraced slopes of the landform are a reminder of the area's mining heritage and serve to stabilize the massive tailings pile.

"After this project, we started thinking, 'What if we were more inventive and brought a designer into the project early?' If we said 'We're going to be moving a billion tons of rock anyway; how would you like us to shape it?' Rather than handle the rock twice, do it once, and do it to the best advantage the first time… Martha certainly opened our eyes to that possibility."

— John McDonough, former Vice President of Environment, Barrick Gold

The Performance of Aesthetics

Interview with Elizabeth K. Meyer

What do you mean when you talk about an aesthetic experience?

If you think about the essential definition of aesthetics, it is not about what something looks like alone, but implies an exchange or a relationship between a viewer, an inhabitant, and a space or a form. The aesthetic experience, then, has to do with the exchange between what you know (your own personal experiences), and what you see. The appearance of something, what it looks like, its shape, its proportions, the way it reminds us of other similar or dissimilar places or forms or spaces— that evokes an emotional, psychological reaction, and that's the performance.

Art historians Arthur Danto and Alexander Nahemas, who have both written about aesthetics, suggest that the experience isn't immediate, because when you see something, it goes back and forth in your brain between conscious and subconscious, awareness and things in the past, what you expect to see or what you have seen before, until what you are seeing registers again. Through this process, the experience is prolonged, even if by a microsecond.

Because of this experience, there is a relationship created between a person and a space, or a painting, or a sculpture, or another person. It is in that moment of recognition that there is the possibility of curiosity, and that curiosity might lead to engagement. There is the possibility of wonder, and that wonder might lead to a sense of connection.

Think of the Exchange Square project in Manchester, for example. As a critic, I can just think about it in terms of what it looks like, but if I went to that place, I would be thinking about it in terms of the IRA bomb and what happened at that site— that project services a much longer history than the trauma of a decade ago; it is really about the endurance of a community. So, someone can look at it and see the references to the history and of the city as if they were random and casual, and yet I think about it in light of the overwhelming association that that part of the city would have to anybody who'd lived through that period. To that community, there is a social sustainability being played out about the resilience of this community over hundreds of years, not several months or a decade.

What about our expectations of what things are supposed to look like? How does this impact the way we relate to public spaces?

There is an assumption in so many people's understanding of beauty that it is constant, that it somehow isn't changing. It is so apparent when you look at other disciplines or at fashion and body types that there are changing conceptions and perceptions of beauty and aesthetics, but there is some misperception that it can't change in landscapes and that those changes can't be connected to the associations that people make with places that they care about or that they know really well.

When Olmsted was talking about the Emerald Necklace in Boston in the 1880s, he said, "I don't really want to call this a park, because it doesn't fill people's expectations of a park, and they might not know what to do with it."

He was really struggling for a way to describe a constructed wetland that wasn't going to look like the Boston Commons or the Public Garden.

This struggle happens frequently where there is a shift in norms.

Different designers use different techniques to make the new resonate. They can't just assume the power of shock the way you could in an art gallery, where visitors are expecting to see something that's going to surprise them. When things are in the public realm, there is a different set of expectations. What's really exciting is when you find a project that is altering one's perception of how a space should be imagined, how it should be experienced, and yet there's something familiar about it that resonates with some cultural expectation from that community or from that city.

Take the Parc des Buttes Chaumont in Paris, for example, which became a park in the 1860s. Before that it was a quarry site, it was a dump, it was where revolutionaries used to be hanged in public display. Yet it was remade into an exhibition for the 1867 Expo in Paris, and it was also a neighborhood park. There are aspects of it that are quite bizarre, yet what is really carefully choreographed is the familiarity of things like the spatial practice of strolling and driving. It was designed so that there was something about the everyday routines of that particular generation that happened within this other surreal space, and so while the forms may have been new and even more exaggerated than in other public parks of the period, the spatial practice was the same. In that case, there were many different associations people had with those forms, and so they weren't only looked at as bizarre quarry remnants. They were understood in relationship to the social history of that as a working-class neighborhood, so the history of labor, the old quarry, and the fact that that was a place where politics have played out—to me, that is a really fascinating project that had a radical impact on people's expectations of that constructed urban landscape.

What is the relationship of the designer to the shaping of these experiences?

A designer has observational skills that are more acute than most people's. We make ourselves crazy seeing things that we see. And that's a gift in a design project: to take that sense, and give it form, and a sense of a place. There is a distillation or condensation of the qualities of a place —it's not a simulation of what's there, it's the representation of it through a lens of someone whose senses are acute. There is something about a poem versus a short story or a novel, which intensifies something that is part of the human condition, but it does so through the juxtaposition of words, the alliteration, the repetition, that is so intensely edited out and succinctly presented that it resonates.

If you're trying to think about the performance of appearance, it works in two ways: There is an interaction, a receptivity that a designer has to the place and then they respond to that and translate it. They distill it. Then, there is something that happens when it is so distilled and intensified that it evokes responses from others, and it's in that evoked response that somebody is connected.

And that's where I think that the power of aesthetics comes in. It is not something that any designer can control or predict, but if you don't deploy your own physical, spatial, visual abilities within a project, you lose out on the unpredictable and marvelous and strange ways in which a project can alter the psychological and emotional experience that people have in a place. I'm happy when places make me healthy physically, but health is more than that. A huge part of health is the connection between the mind and the body, and the mind needs to have jolts of things besides fresh air and clean water, and one of them is wonder and awe and surprise and the job that comes from experiencing an unexpected solution to what seems to be a quite normal place or everyday place.

Why is this so critical in today's urban environments?

Landscapes need an incredible amount of love. They need buy-in, management, care, and that happens when somebody in a community feels connected to a place.

If people are walking by the totally invisible but highly responsible rain garden or bioswale, it never occurs to them that that was a constructed thing, that it needs anyone to care for it. Landscapes that are striking visually, that are clearly constructed, have the potential to engender a sense of connection and care and a community that will in fact want to be involved in them for a long time.

None of these projects can assume that the few people who are around when it was designed are going to be there for the long haul to actually buy into it. You want to make sure that every generation, every new year of students to a university or every new group of neighbors to a community, can also engage with it. That does not just come from an innate care for the environment (which a lot of people don't have), but from other sources, like the excitement that comes from an aesthetic experience, the way that the project challenges you, the way it takes you out of your everyday experience or jolts you into a new relationship with the place. It makes you wonder why something is the way it is and how that connects with something else. The immediate benefit is just the joy of being in the moment living, and the longer-term impact is that it starts to build relationships and connections to place, and through that extension, a commitment to caring and to managing and maintaining that place.

03.

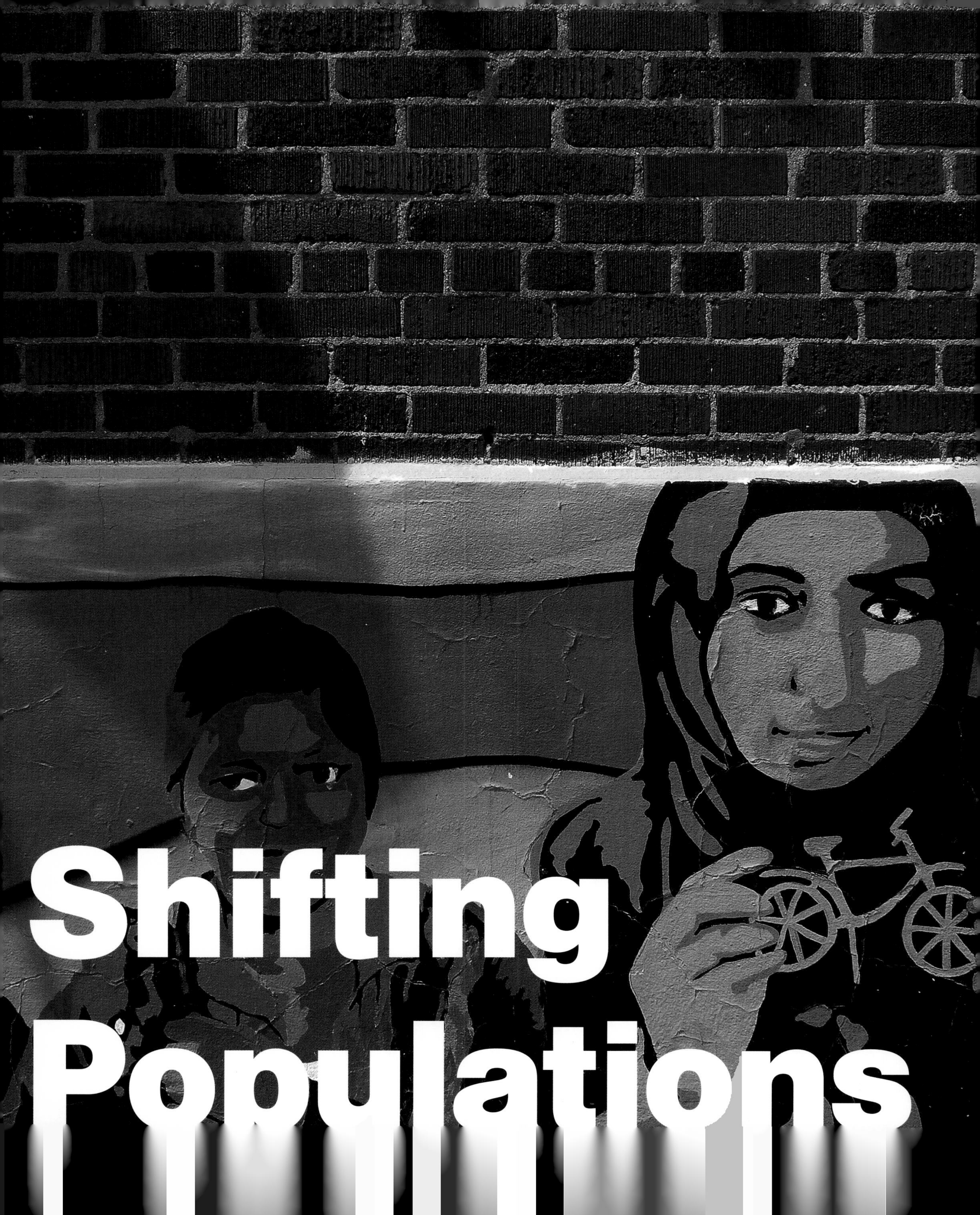
Shifting
Populations

When populations leave one place, they arrive in another. As some cities grow and diversify with international immigration and rural migration from within their own countries, other cities are left with diminished populations and unbalanced demographics. These cities must adapt. Rapidly expanding urban areas must adjust to accommodate higher densities and multiple cultures, while shrinking cities must diversify their offers to reverse the trends of out-migration.

From left: The Greek City of Edessa, Edessa, Greece; Abu Dhabi Corniche Beach, Abu Dhabi, UAE; Central Park Monte Laa, Vienna, Austria.

Levi's

Central Park Monte Laa

Before a surge of immigration in the 1990s brought a large and diverse population to Vienna's already dense Tenth District, the site that is now the Monte Laa neighborhood, was an eight-lane highway carrying passengers into and out of Vienna from the south.

Top: Monte Laa neighborhood festival, 2009. Bottom: Relaxing in wooden lounge chairs.

Austria's unique geographical position, wedged between Eastern and Western Europe, has supported the country's role as a transitory migration point between the two halves of the continent, and has produced its diverse population of immigrants from across Eastern Europe, the Balkans, Turkey, and Germany.

After decades of population loss following the Second World War, Austria grew rapidly throughout the 1980s and early 1990s. The fall of the Iron Curtain in 1989 and the beginning of the Yugoslav Wars in 1991 began a surge of immigration from the east across the Austrian border and into the capital city of Vienna. During that period, the number of non-nationals living in Austria doubled, and by 2001, at least 12.5 percent of the country's population was foreign-born, compared to 11.8 percent of the United States population at the same time.[1]

The quickly rising population spawned a wave of renewal activity to meet the overwhelming demand for subsidized housing. The growth plan followed Vienna's famous model of "soft urban renewal." Instead of wholesale redevelopment, which leads to gentrification and inflated housing prices, deteriorating housing stocks and aging infrastructure are incrementally improved. As rents and housing prices remain stable, neighborhood residents continue to be able to afford their homes, guaranteeing a desired income mix in districts across the city.[2]

Aerial photograph illustrates the rigid boundaries around Vienna's growth area.

Vienna's long-held policy to avoid sprawl, and to preserve its more than 50 percent green space coverage, focused all of the development of the 1990s into designated in-town expansion areas, where they selectively replace inadequate buildings and find new opportunities for density through innovative infill schemes. Much of the new growth would be absorbed by the city's most heavily populated Tenth District. The new neighborhood of Monte Laa was planned here at the southeast threshold of the city's development boundary, where dense urban fabric quickly gives way to the agricultural plots that spread beyond the Hungarian border to the east.

The new mixed-used neighborhood would be developed on opposite sides of the A22 highway, one of two primary entrances to Vienna from the south. The new 800-unit development was intended to connect the dense Favoriten neighborhood to the northwest with the popular Laaer Wald recreation area to the southeast.

"The idea was quite utopian. How can you create a compact city where there is no separation between all of the different uses like working, living, and leisure? The park was the element that could bring everything together."

— Albert Wimmer, Master Plan Architect

The A22 highway is bridged with a huge concrete slab to connect the neighborhoods on either side of the highway.

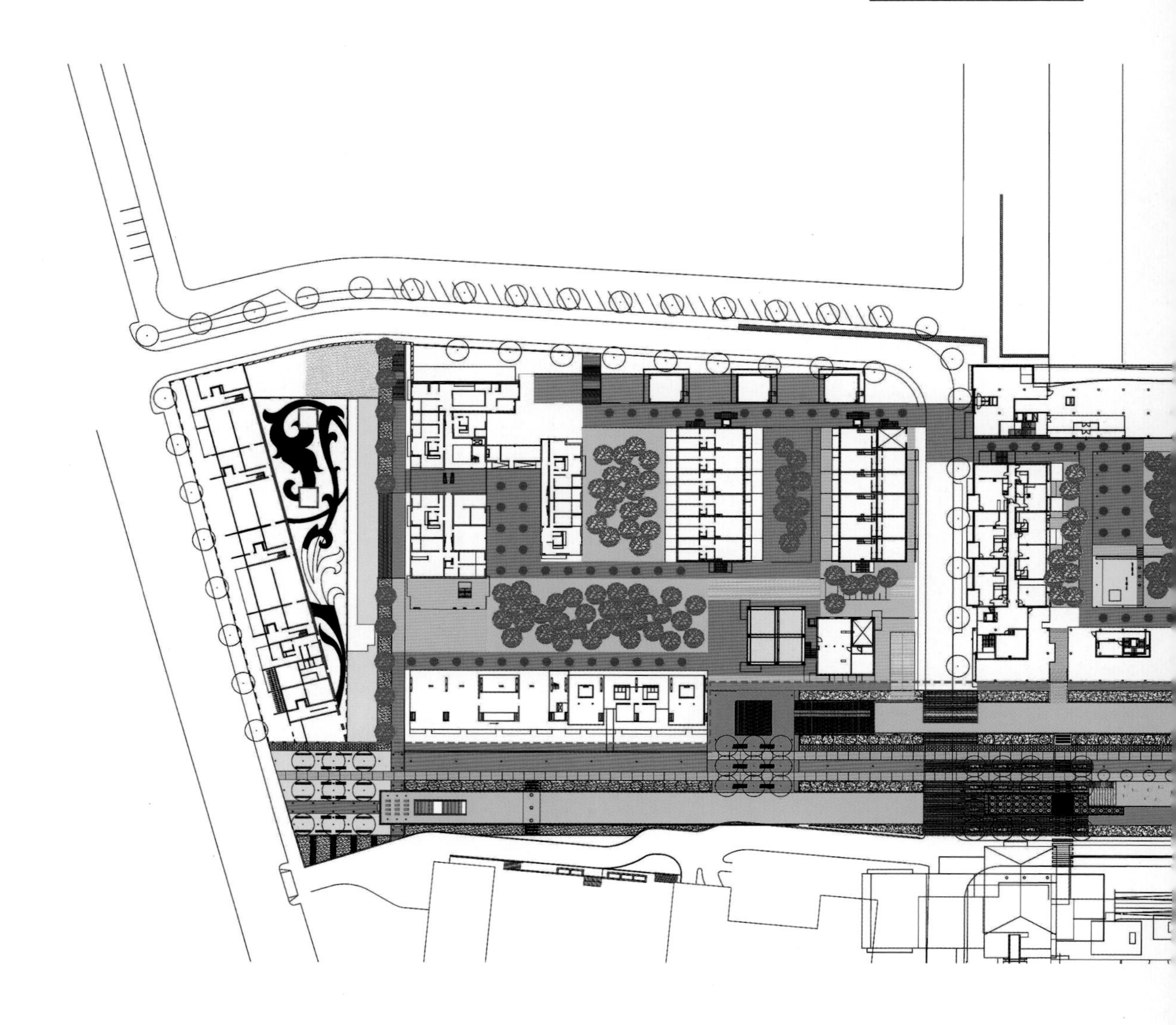

A Compact City

Albert Wimmer, Hans Hollein, and Martha Schwartz Partners' winning scheme for the Monte Laa neighborhood master plan stretched a huge slab over the highway that would literally connect the two areas on either side.

Their proposal for a "compact city" was fixed around a linear central park designed by Martha Schwartz Partners. On one side were 800 residential units, and on the other were all of the remaining functions of the city—an elementary school, offices, shops, restaurants, and transit. The park,

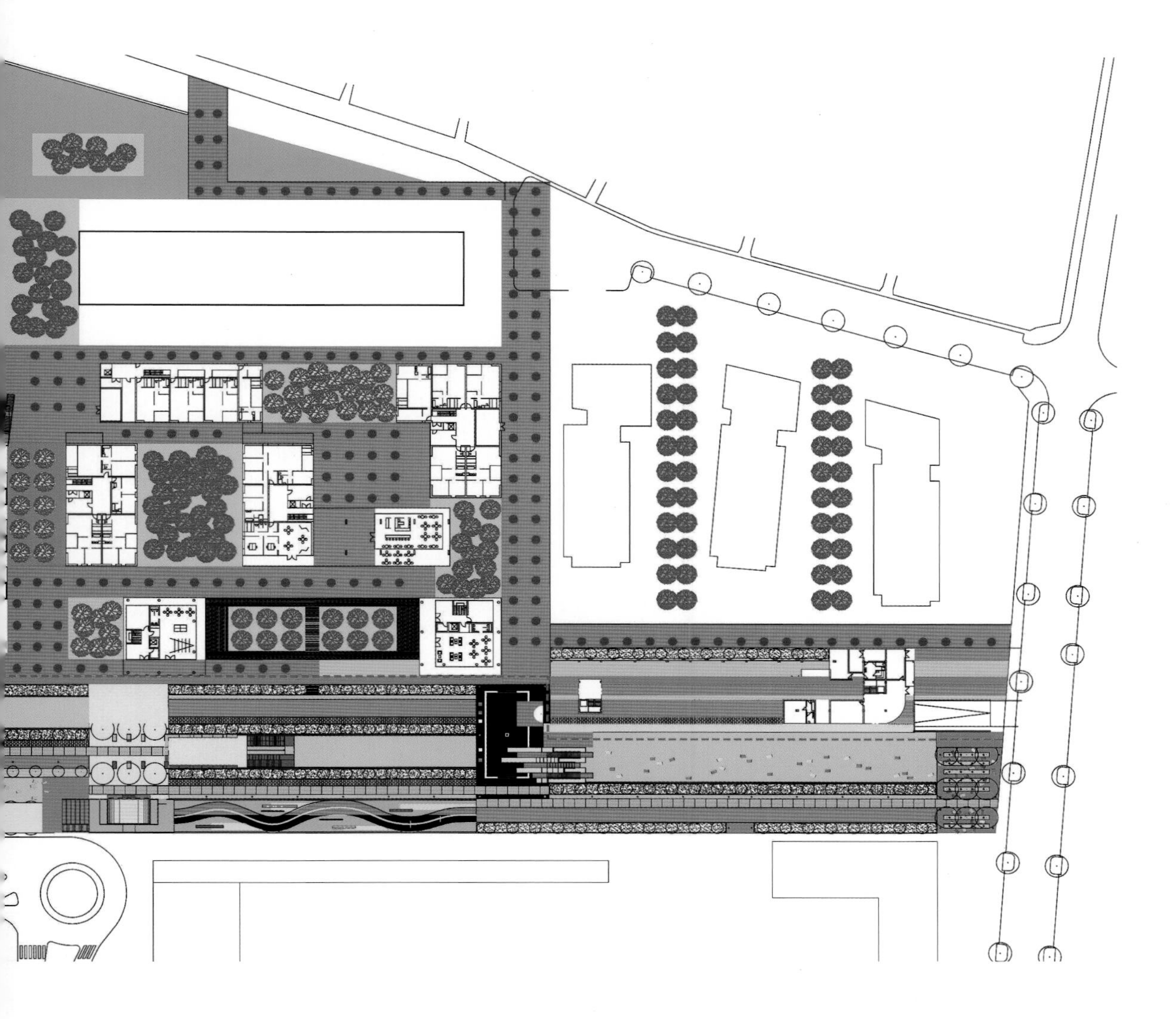

which is completely open to the public, would be the connective tissue between the two, providing the primary open space for the young immigrant families and office workers in the area.

The challenge for the designers was to accommodate such a diverse population and range of uses in this condensed urban space.

Site plan, not to scale.

Schwartz used her experience growing up near Fairmount Park in Philadelphia as a cautionary tale of the complexities of designing public space in a diverse urban environment:
"Fairmount Park was an open, green, pastoral space that was designed to serve everyone, but that meant there were no designated spaces and no real way to define your own territory. This 'democratic' approach to public space planning has not worked in most urban contexts, where so many different people have to share one space. What happened in Fairmount Park was that the guys with the biggest bats got to control the place. Public spaces work best when a bigger space is subdivided into smaller spaces where people can find their own niches that feel defensible. They can occupy the one big space together, but still stay within their own group and comfort zone. Then the adventurous few on the frontlines of the integration process can venture forth and regroup as they wish."

The central park is divided into many smaller areas to serve a dense and diverse population.

Smaller Spaces to Make a Larger Whole

The Monte Laa Central Park is designed with that principle in mind. It offers one larger space divided into smaller spaces where people can choose how and where they occupy the park. Between the 800 housing units, the offices, and the school, more than 2,000 people would be relying on this small piece of land as their primary open space. It had to be diverse enough to meet the social and physical needs of the different groups, but also cohesive enough to hold the compact new neighborhood together.

The designers achieved this complex (and seemingly conflicting) ambition with three strategies. Each of the strategies, while serving to parcel the 400-meter site, is repeated across the length of the park to create a unified understanding of the space as a whole.

Corresponding Front Lawns

To give building residents a sense of ownership over part of the space, each of the buildings facing the park was accorded its own corresponding section of green space, which is defined by a break in the linear green surface. The breaks become walkways and roadways for pedestrians and cars to cross from the residences on one side of the park to the offices, schools, and restaurants on the other side.

Although the whole length of the park is public, the relationship of each building to its own section of the space gives residents a front lawn that feels like an extension of their lives within the building. Parents feel confident allowing their young children out to play floors below because they can see that they are safe within the well-defined boundaries of the front lawn space.

Each building has its own corresponding section of the central park.

"The neighborhood has a strong community, and the public realm is becoming part of their personal environments. They host events there. They spend time here. They have really taken it over as their own."

— Albert Wimmer, Master Plan Architect

The playground area, designed to accommodate all different age groups, attracts children from within the neighborhood and also from the surrounding districts.

Topographical Platforms

The second organizing element works with the site's sloping topography, which drops almost 12 meters as it moves from the southeast to the northwest end of the space. As the park slopes down, a series of ramps slope up in the opposite direction, mitigating the sense of the overall grade change while providing a diverse set of elements to support an even more diverse range of activities. The ramps vary in length and height, and each comes to an end with a different urban element to connect the upper edge of the slope back down to ground level. One ramp ends with oversized amphitheater seating where teenagers can hang out and gossip, children can climb, and audiences can gather for neighborhood events or outdoor performances.

Another ramp ends with double-wide slides, big enough to encourage group sliding on a busy day. Yet another is strewn with moveable wooden lounge chairs for people to gather in conversation, or for a solitary read in the sun. All of the elements of the park consider the large population of young children in the neighborhood and invite playing, jumping, climbing, sliding, and exploration, while also remembering that their parents need grown-up-sized places to sit and mingle with one another.

Because of the two different sides of the ramps, the park offers different faces to the streets at either end of the site. From the city end of the park that leads toward the Laaer Wald recreation area, views open to a lush, green park space. Walking toward the city end, the space presents a harder, urban face with stepped seating, playgrounds, fountains, and performance spaces. It provides two parks in one and helps to connect the previously disparate districts of the city.

Aerial view of topographic platforms shows the different urban elements at the end of each slope.

Multiple Spaces and Multiple Programs

At the ground level, the surface of the park is broken down into multiple smaller spaces, some similar and some very different in size and program, each offering endless opportunities for different forms of colonization. A shallow fountain invites children to splash and play, barefoot teenagers to flirt on a romantic stroll, or dogs to dash through to cool their paws on a hot day. A half-pipe and basketball courts cater to the teenage crowd and have become a big attraction for kids across the tenth district. Different types and arrangements of seating also offer varieties of occupation. From painted pink logs, to isolated wooden benches, to a whole plaza full of granite seating blocks, everyone in Monte Laa can find a space to sit and to define as his or her own. Taken together, the multiple small spaces combine to create a unified whole, serving the larger community for neighborhood gatherings, summer festivals, and performances.

The linear park is broken down into many smaller areas each with endless possibilities for sitting, playing, or hanging out.

BURTON

Starting A Process

The process of integrating into a new country, a new city, or even a new neighborhood takes time. If we strive to understand this intensified condition, open space and park design can adapt to new populations and to new uses over time and can become the mixing points of the city. At Monte Laa, the central park has become an active participant in that process, providing a place where people can be individuals as part of a larger collective.

"One of the main questions we had to address with this project was: How do you help people to arrange themselves when they start living in an area? Design is one thing, but what is actually interesting is how you get the integration process going—the process of taking on the city as your own. This doesn't happen over one or two years; it is ongoing. Over time, at Monte Laa that feeling is getting stronger, and the park is getting richer."

— Albert Wimmer, Master Plan Architect

Achilles

The Greek City of Edessa

This studio deals with an increasingly difficult issue: small cities losing populations and, as a result, large cities gaining them. Throughout the term, students will address the economic, cultural, and environmental issues that arise when small cities lose essential population, while at the same time, larger cities are unable to assume the influx of migrants.

Professor Martha Schwartz
Department of
Landscape Architecture

Professor Spiro Pollalis
Department of Architecture

Studio Participants
Abhishek Sharma
Angeliki Evripioti
Braham Ketcham
Chandrani Majumdar
Jessica Wolff
John Pawlak
Julian Wu
Milee Shrestha
Nan Cao Chen II
Pao Chun Chen
Richa Shukla
Shane Zhao
Wendy Smith

GSD studio trip to Edessa, September 2009.

The Edessa Region

Edessa, located in the northwest areas of Greece's Macedonia region, is an ancient small town located 120 kilometers northwest of Thessalonica in northern Greece. Its closest international borders are with former Yugoslav Republic of Macedonia, Albania, and Bulgaria.

Edessa is one of many small hill towns situated in the forested Edesseos river valley that flows south from Lake Vegoritida and the Agras Nissi Vritta wetlands. Edessa sits at the edge of a plateau overlooking the Plains of Helles that extend east to Thessalonica. From the edge of this plateau, the rivers fall spectacularly 70 meters down from the ledge to the plain below. These waterfalls are a well-known and celebrated natural feature that has drawn people to Edessa for hundreds of years.

Known historically as the "City of Water," the town boasts an intricate system of waterways—canals, rivulets, and waterfalls—intertwined with small streets, walking paths, and scenic overlooks. This public realm, although scenic, suffers from inattention and minimal investment; existing infrastructure cannot support the concomitant spatial demands of tourism, such as hotels, restaurants, and parking.

As with many agricultural towns in the Macedonian region and in many such regions globally, their natural beauty belies a precarious economic future. As their economies shift away from agriculture, they are quickly losing both their economic and population bases.

In order to keep a population of mixed ages and to successfully develop a service economy, Edessa will have to choose a strategy that will generate a new economy and at the same time protect their natural environment. Can a new strategy of catalytic urban landscape investments improve the internal structure of the town? Can it connect it better to the larger region to create a new economy that will serve the citizens for the next century?

The studio investigates opportunities for the town of Edessa relative to its socio-spatial role in the larger region, its potential as a tourist destination, and its unique riverine ecology. At a regional scale, the viability of predominantly agrarian small towns is at the center of this investigation.

Landscapes of Urbanization: From the Region to the Site

The studio will investigate the repositioning of Edessa at a range of scales, including regional, metropolitan, and specific site design strategies. Products include overall development and open space plans for the region, as well as the design of a very specific and comparatively large open space in the heart of the town. This space is considered a catalyst to the overall redevelopment agenda. The studio incorporates broad planning and environmental management approaches, as well as detailed design.

Goals of the studio investigation:

- To determine a development strategy for Edessa that will reposition the city and regenerate its economy and population
- To develop an economic strategy, program, and land-use plan for development, including the design and development of the central open space (stadium site)
- To create a synergy between the two towns in the valley that are connected by the river
- To capture the full potential of the river valley (both above and below the falls) while protecting it for the future
- To determine highest value and best land uses in the river/greenway area
- To improve internal connections throughout the town of Edessa via a public open-space system to the greenway and to Agras
- To understand how (or whether) to integrate Edessa into a "global" economy: How might Edessa brand itself, potentially using the redeveloped public realm as a selling point?

Questions for investigation:

- How can landscape and infrastructure design work together to address the demands of connectivity and increased capacity while also provoking a sense of identity and "place" for a small town?
- How can issues of sustainability and environmental stewardship be calibrated to the specifics of local culture and geography?
- How can recent shifts in the regional geopolitical sphere be actuated to bolster tourism and economic development?
- How can strategic investments in landscape and infrastructure be leveraged to provide development opportunity both at the scale of the town and for the larger region?

The Edessa region and its landscapes.

Analysis and Observations

Population

While it may appear that over the past 30 years, Edessa has had a strong rate of population growth, the present growth rate is 0.46%, indicating that the trends of the past have grown stagnant.

Waterfalls

- Most visitors to Edessa come by car, but there are no dedicated parking facilities at the waterfalls.
- Tour buses drop off at the waterfalls, park offsite, and then return for pick-up.
- Many private tour bus operations only stop at the waterfalls, and therefore pass the city of Edessa altogether.
- Of the visitors to the waterfalls, 74 percent are Greek citizens, and 65–70 percent are families.
- Visitors are mainly interested in the waterfall, park, open air, museum, and Varosi.
- Waterfalls are open 24 hours a day, every day.
- Standard park benches provide little seating.
- There is a consistent use of materials: flagstone, engineered stone composite paving, brick, and metal.
- There is existing initiative to draw people to special attractions at night with lighting displays on the waterfalls.

Sewage System

- The sewage system in Edessa is almost 450 years old. It is beginning to show signs of degradation and might not be able to meet today's demands for long.
- Before the 1950s, Edessa's wastewater was discharged directly into canals and rivers, which then flowed over the waterfalls.
- In the 1950s, a vertical canal sewer along the cliff edge was introduced, separating wastewater from the canals and waterfalls.
- The canals still function as a drainage system for the city, collecting rainwater and some wastewater.

Wastewater Treatment:

- A new biological wastewater treatment plant treats wastewater from Edessa and several other towns before it goes into the irrigation system.

Waste Management:

- Currently there is no waste recycling management in Edessa and other surrounding towns.
- The local landfill has capacity for 15 more years.

Water Supply and Consumption:

- Karkagia Spring is the only water source for the city of Edessa. It has very high-quality potable water that requires little treatment before going into the city supply lines.
- There is no measurement of its total capacity.
- Water consumption in Edessa is estimated at 1 million cubic meters per year, but due to the poor management system, the actual water consumption in the municipality of Edessa could possibly be as high as 2 million cubic meters.
- The water supply is not well managed, as potable water from Karkagia is used for irrigation, as well.

Energy Management:
- Energy supply is managed by the Public Power Corporation of Greece.
- Electricity comes from the national electricity network.
- Two hydroelectricity power plants operate near Edessa.
- Water is induced from Lake Vergoritis and Agras wetland to the power plant to generate electric power. Due to the decrease of water level in Lake Vergoritis, the canal from the lake to the power plant doesn't work anymore.
- The power plants in the area run only three or four hours per day in peak season. The power generated from the power plants is sent to national electricity grids instead of to Edessa.

Ecological Threats:
- Soil erosion and overuse are threats.
- There is a high flooding risk, due to an existing dam that broke once in 1975.
- Increasing fisheries and orchards could pollute the water in the valley, even though it would bring an economy to the area. One suggestion is to implement organic farming and a cleansing wetland system for the pollution path before it gets to the lake.

Open Space Experience:
- In the small village of Agras to the west, residents do not use the valley open space due to its poor condition.
- Agras also had a beautiful waterfall on its east edge in the valley that provided a completely different experience from the waterfall at Edessa.
- The waterfall of Edessa is 75 meters high and has a monumental scale. Historically, the waterfall of Agras was a series of four cascading waterfalls 4 to 8 meters high that ultimately drop into a 30-meter-high waterfall.
- The use of Edessios River for electricity generation since the 1950s led to the demise of Agras Waterfall, along with its potential for any aquatic habitat.
- One could visualize Edessa and Agras as a part of one system with a 2-kilometer valley stretch of natural resources in between; presently, the only anchor point for the visitors are the Edessa Waterfall.

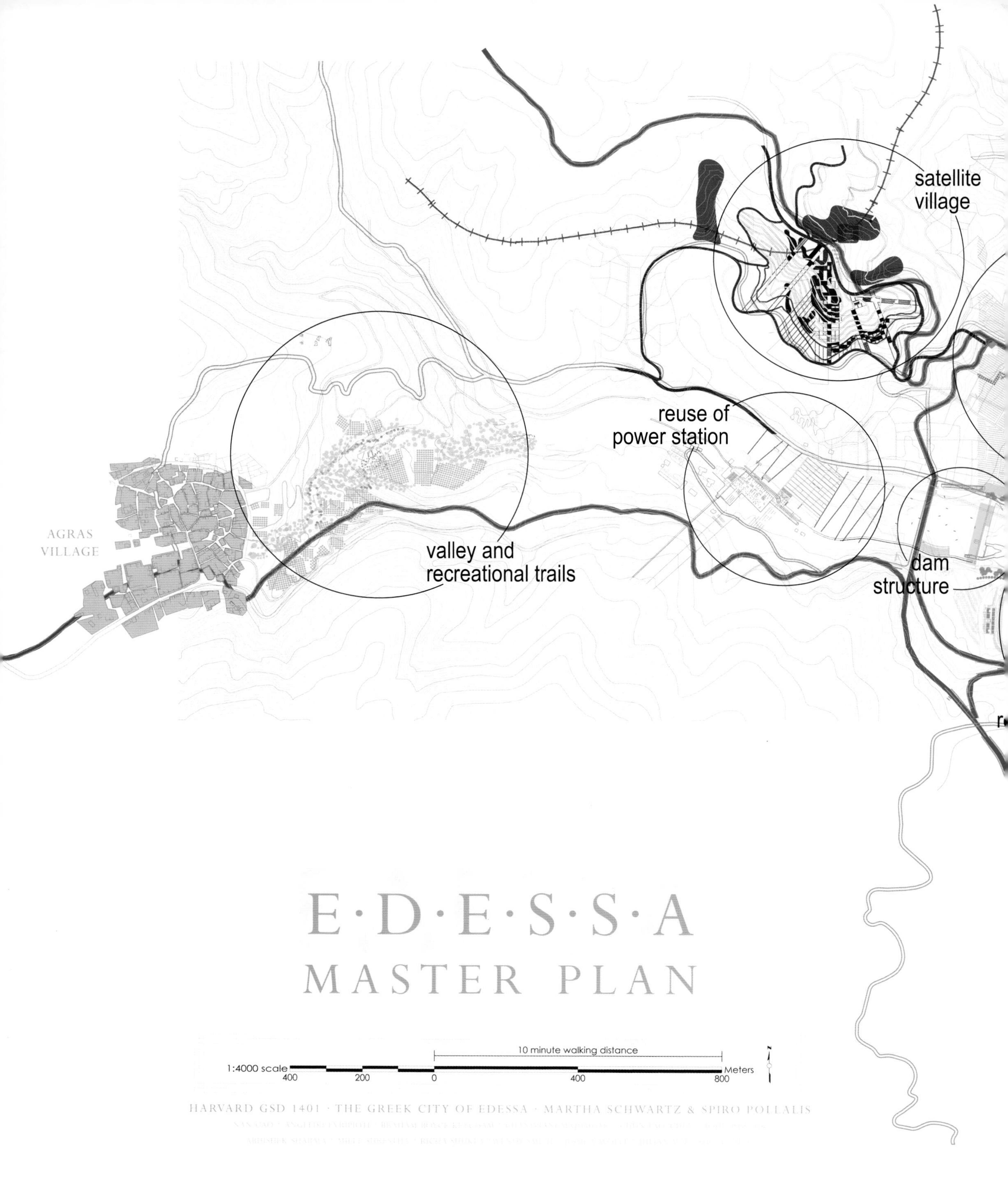
satellite
village
reuse of
power station
AGRAS
VILLAGE
valley and
recreational trails
dam
structure
E·D·E·S·S·A
MASTER PLAN
10 minute walking distance
1:4000 scale
400
200
0
400
800
Meters
HARVARD GSD 1401 · THE GREEK CITY OF EDESSA · MARTHA SCHWARTZ & SPIRO POLLALIS

The Masterplan is a product of the entire studio. Each student then focussed on one area of the plan to propose a design intervention.

Jessica Wolff & Julian Wu

Lower Edessa Valley Recreational Corridor

In Edessa, Greece, the love of sports is evident, but there is a dearth of available facilities and open spaces in which city dwellers may find comfort being active. A "recreational corridor" park project could provide Edessians with the opportunity to participate in a variety of athletic activities, and also be a spectator. The recreational corridor park will be a network of woven pathways that connect across the lower valley to different "nodes," such as a proposed soccer stadium, lake, and agricultural park area.

Abhishek Sharma

Night Park & AquaCulture Farm

This project is based upon expanding Edessa's night life and inserting an art facility that will attract artists and create a base for recreational and cultural activities that will attract both citizens of and visitors to Edessa. The site is envisioned to become a night park that indulges the people of Edessa and surrounding villages after work and into the evening. The park also has a working layer, as it performs as an aquaculture farm.

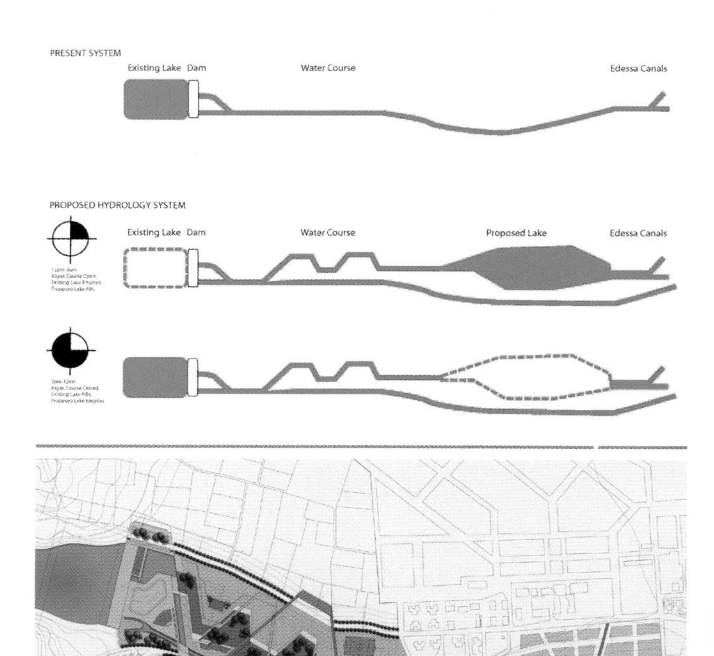

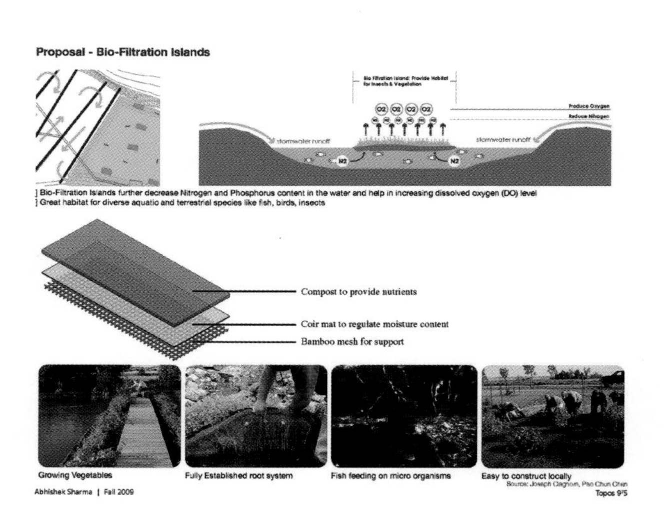

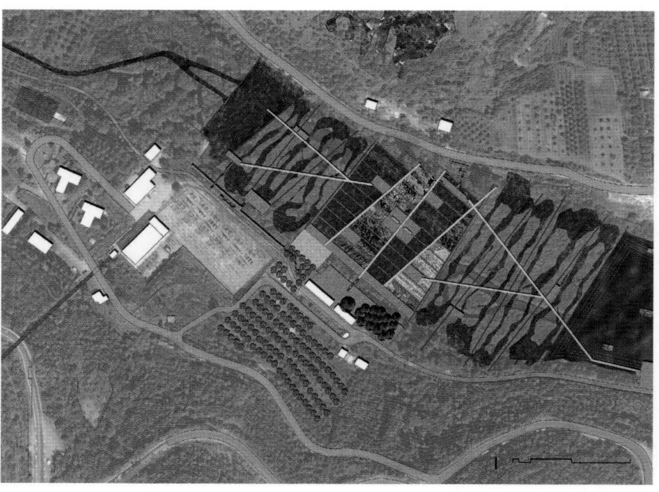

Angeliki Evripioti

Satellite Village

The plan proposes the creation of a satellite village to accommodate new development, while preserving an agricultural band close to the city core. As the city looks to the future and plans for growth in population and city extent, it must consider how and where it can accommodate new development. The village will be roughly 1 kilometer from the existing city, which is still within walking distance, so the new village will have a strong connection to the city.

Richa Shukla & John Pawlak

Agri-tourism & Processing Plant
Stimulus to the Agricultural Valley of Edessa

Edessa must expand its vision beyond tourism in order to create a more stable and sustainable economy for the city. The project will introduce agri-tourism to the valley, collectivize the cherry farms and farmers so to enable more production and distribution of a very highly prized local product, encourage tourism by organizing the celebration of the cherry industry of Edessa through the creation of an Edessa Cherry Festival, and reinforce the image of the city by encouraging more cherry tree planting on a civic scale.

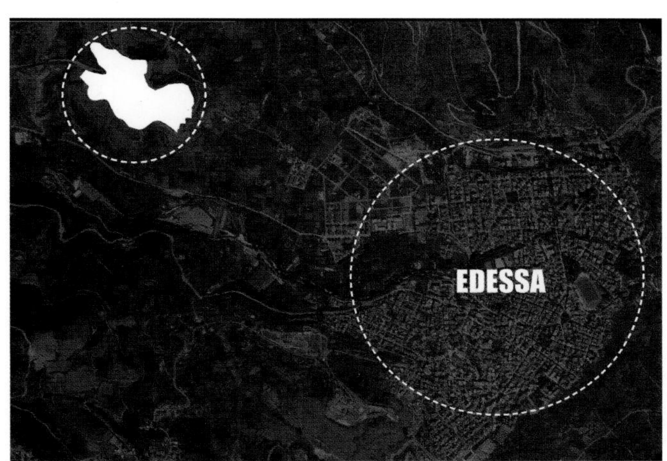

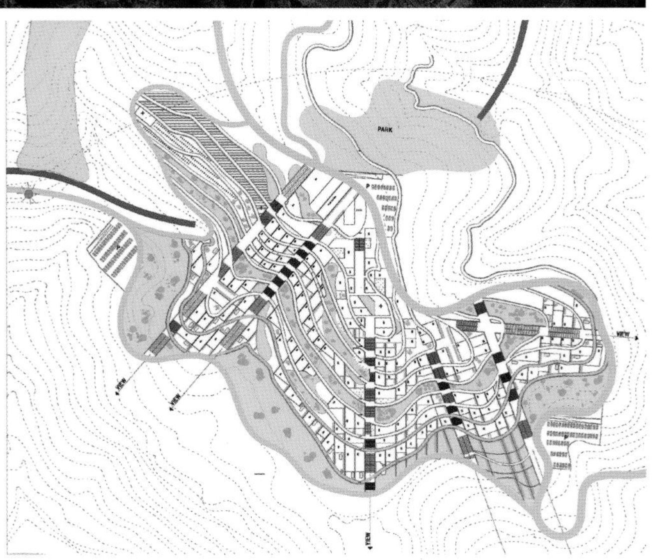

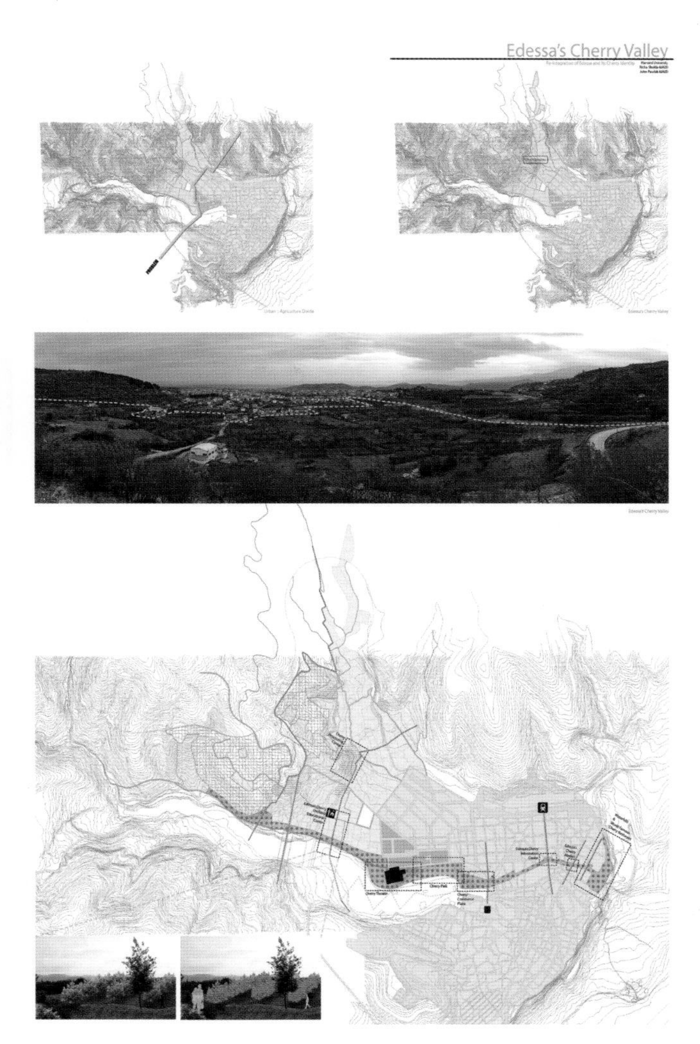

Chandrani Majumdar & Milee Shrestha

Agras Falls and Pools

This project proposes to establish a second anchor point in Agras by reopening Agras Waterfall and tapping into existing resources for economic regeneration. Reopening the waterfall is also envisioned as a catalyst for the redesign of Karkagya, which is the drinking water spring for Edessa and the stream corridor connection between Karkagya and Agras.

Pao Chun Chen

A New Public Park in the Heart of Edessa

This project aims to provide the city of Edessa with an occupation-worthy and economically sustainable plaza that accommodates rich program and becomes the new front door to the city for tourists. Moreover, a parking garage that will accommodate more than 600 cars will be designed under the plaza to supplement the city's current deficiency of parking for the crowds of tourists it wishes to attract.

perspective view: soccer field + exterior look of culture center

Nan Cao

Stairway Parks from Tsitsi Park to the Archeological Site

The unique value of Edessa lies not only in its waterfall, but also in the elements of the city behind the waterfall—that is, the cliff edge or the "brow." Expanded opportunities to explore the brow and cliff edge will add to the existing tourist attractions of the town. But because of this new way of exploring the city and the magnificent view over the plain, visitors' time in Edessa will be extended, bringing with it increased revenue.

Shane Zhao

The Edessa Dam Project

Situated at the nexus between Edessa and Agras will be the future site of a new anchor point that will serve to amplify the economic viability of Edessa's future urban corridor. Strategically located at the junction between all vital organs of the proposed master plan, the site in focus is a new dam complex that will stand as a pedestrian hotspot. Both in its figurative expression and programmatic function, the new complex will perform as a keystone in the transformation of Edessa's urban corridor into a premiere recreational destination.

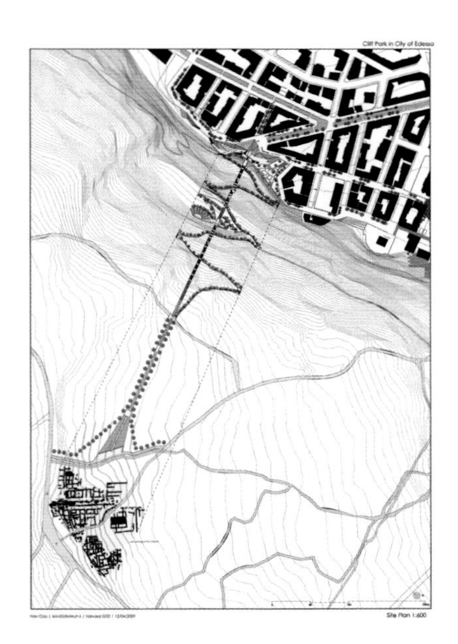

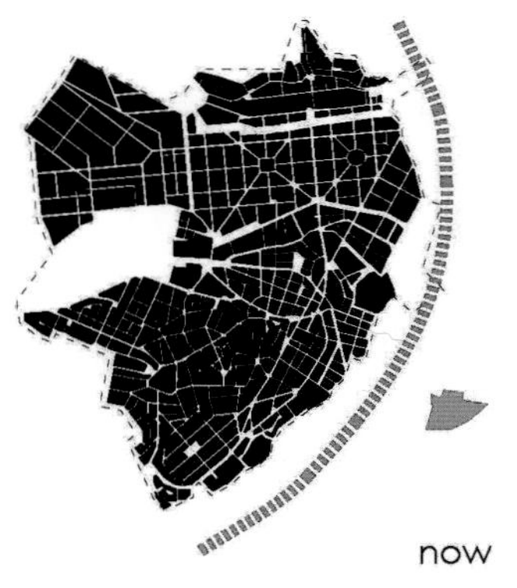

Wendy Smith
Falls Swimming Park

A more legible falls area will better tie the area to the other tourist attractions immediately associated with it: The "brow," the new soccer field, the historic city of Varosi, Tsitsi Park and the cliff face, and the archaeological ruins below. The design of walkways, meadows, and swimming opportunities will enhance the spectacle and the proximity of water in a new public landscape that will impel people to stay at least overnight, if not longer.

"Over the years, I have had the pleasure of working with many scientists, planners, urban designers, architects, and engineers. What I received from these professionals was usually a coherent outlook, but it more often than not had inherent limitations. What I understood when we took on the Harvard Studio was that these studies and exercises of Edessa did not require and should not require any limitations or safeguards. What was needed was a free, unlimited, unrestricted expression that could often result in crazy or absurd ideas, which could then be refined, contextualized, and formatted as required.

The studies confirmed many issues and also paved the way for other issues to be explored. They confirmed the need to have a coherent master plan for the town of Edessa and its region. They confirmed the need for a new approach with regard to policymaking and dealing with the future development of the town.

Prior to the studio, I had a narrow mind-set when I thought about how Edessa could be developed. It was through this collaboration that I came to understand that nothing was impossible."

— Ioannis Sontras, Former Mayor of Edessa

Master Plan

Education

Establish an educational base to attract and retain young people

Establishing a new university branch in Edessa is a central pillar of this plan. With university students come vibrant street life, night-time activities, and stimulus for the local economy.

Goal 1: Establish a new university branch in Edessa
This plan envisions a new university branch of a sufficient size to stimulate the growth of the city and provide a new independent base for the city's overall economy. After an initial period of growth, a total student population of between 800 and 1,000 will help to create a strong sense of student culture and youthful vitality in the city, without overwhelming the city or making the economy overly dependent upon the education sector.

For this goal to reinforce several of the other goals presented in this plan, the new university branch should focus primarily on environmental studies and ecological management. In this way, the entire valley may become a classroom for the students, and the university would become a stakeholder in the responsible preservation of the city's natural surroundings.

The establishment of this university branch would serve several important functions for the city. First, universities create jobs at all levels, from low-level staff to highly educated professorial positions. Second, students bring discretionary spending, which stimulates the local retail economy. And perhaps most importantly, the establishment of a significant student population could help to offset Edessa's brain drain, as qualified young people leave the city in their twenties and don't return until they are much older and past their peak of productivity.

Goal 2: Stimulate the economy by attracting resident students who will remain through holidays and summers
Although Edessa already has one university branch – a department of management and administration affiliated with the Aristotle University of Thessaloniki – it doesn't create a sufficient number of year-round student residents to create significant effects for the local economy. Of the roughly 200 current students, only about half keep a residence in Edessa, and many of those leave for holidays and the summer.

Therefore, the proposed new university branch should be of a sufficient size to create a core population of students who remain in the city year-round. This would help to create a more stable population base for the city, so the benefits of having students, especially in terms of cultural activities and other events, would persist throughout the year, and there wouldn't be any down time when the city feels like a less active place to be. Furthermore, we anticipate that students who stay over the holidays may bring their relatives to visit the city, as well.

Goal 3: Integrate the university with the city
The proposed university will not follow the model of an American-style campus. Instead, the buildings of the university will be fully integrated into the city-center. The growth plan for the university is to begin with one university building in each of the two new city-centers to help anchor the linear axis of the city. As the city grows, a third building could go in the southeastern corner of the city, emphasizing a north-south axis that runs to the train station.

Goal 4: Disperse student housing throughout the city
An additional goal to help distribute the positive effects of a university throughout the city will be to disperse student housing throughout the city. Rather than relying on dormitories, students will live in apartment buildings in the current city, as well as in the proposed growth area to the northwest of the city. This will help stimulate the housing market within the city, and it will ensure that the students are full participants in the life of the city, rather than being consigned to one small part of it.

Tourism

Capture overnight domestic tourists and begin to market Edessa to the international market
As Edessa looks to create new sustainable economic bases, the expansion of tourism presents a clear opportunity. Edessa is well positioned to capture greater benefits from tourism. This plan envisions the increased emphasis on tourism not as the sole engine of Edessa's economy, but as one element in a multi-pronged development approach.

Goal 1: Create a new focus on ecotoursim and outdoor recreational activites
The greatest change to Edessa's tourism strategy will be the addition of new local activities that will make the city more attractive to visitors. These activities are developed from Edessa's untapped strengths: new recreational opportunities will make use of the high-quality outdoor spaces and agri-tourism will be supported by the local agricultural base.

Goal 2: Promote Edessa's distinctive characteristics: its waterfalls, the archaeological sites, and its unique history
Key to Edessa's overall tourism message will be the explicit promotion of what makes the city distinctive: its unique mix of natural features, archaeological sites, historical development patterns, and the vibrant city-center. This combination of features can add up to a compelling narrative about what the city as a whole has to offer.

Goal 3: Position Edessa as the center of a network of year-round destinations
Edessa can also improve its tourist industry by positioning itself as the regional base for a variety of outdoor activities throughout northern Greece. This could help to offset any seasonal fluctuations in local tourism, as Edessa would be able to become a year-round destination. For example, outdoor recreational activities in the immediate vicinity could be supplemented by visitors who go skiing in the mountains to the northwest and visit the thermal baths. These visitors could be encouraged to stay at hotels in Edessa and travel to the ski slopes as a day trip.

This approach would eventually change the way that domestic tourists in particular view Edessa. Rather than just thinking of Edessa as a place to visit during the summer travel season, the city could become a destination for all four seasons.

Goal 4: Convert Edessa from a single-day tourist stop into an overnight destination
The city must work to capture overnight guests out of the existing number of tourists who come for the waterfalls.

By expanding the tourism base in the ways described in the other goals, the city can broaden its overall appeal, which will help it to attract more tourists and may convince many to stay overnight.

Because the overall volume of annual tourists is quite high because of the waterfall, at about 750,000 visitors, the city only needs to convert a small percentage of these visitors to overnight stays for them to see significant benefits. For example, because the city currently has about 600 beds right now, capturing just 3 percent of the visitors for overnight stays would require the addition of 60 more beds, or a 10 percent growth in the city's hotel industry.

Goal 5: Create a consistent branded identity for the city through marketing
Finally, the city must create a unified marketing strategy centered around a strong brand identity. The posters pictured here are illustrative of one concept that could help the city pitch itself as a sum of a number of diverse elements and attractions. This strategy could be multi-pronged, and promoted through many types of media.

Phasing And Road Network

Goal 1: Change the street grid and housing typology in the existing Smareka neighborhood to create higher density
The Smareka neighborhood is the site of the most recent housing developments in Edessa. The neighborhood has several large single-family houses, laid out on a street grid with an extremely large block structure. Luckily, much of the land remains vacant and undeveloped, so it may

be possible to alter the trajectory of the area before it is completed.

First, and perhaps most importantly, the city must encourage all future development in this area to take place at a much higher density than it has so far. The surrounding hills with steep slopes mean that the Smareka location is the last flat land adjacent to the city of significant size that may be developed. Therefore, it is imperative that the area be developed in a way that makes the most of this opportunity. Because the neighborhood is so close to the expanded canal and urban waterfront area, it seems likely that the neighborhood will be able to support the higher density of development, even including the low-density housing that has already been built.

But in addition, the street grid must be altered so the blocks are on a more human scale than they are today. The current blocks—which are nearly superblocks—should be divided by building new, smaller roads and footpaths through the blocks, to extend the urban fabric from the rest of the city.

Goal 2: One option: encourage future growth in the nearby villages
Because of the constraints of the natural topography, Edessa's physical expansion will necessarily be limited in the near future. To preserve the essential character of the existing city, we propose that one option for future growth would be to encourage the further development of the three villages that are in close proximity to Edessa. By shifting the growth to these areas, Edessa becomes the center of a loose network of walkable towns, but it still can retain the feel of a smaller city.

Goal 3: Another option: create a satellite city on the hill to the northwest of the city
After the Smareka neighborhood is more fully developed, the city will once again need to identify land that it can expand to. As already outlined, the preservation of an agricultural belt will push the next round of development farther away from the existing city. Therefore, we propose that the city build a satellite village or node on the hill that lies northwest of the city. The peak of this hill is roughly 1 kilometer from the existing city, which is still within walking distance, so the new village will have a strong connection to the city.

Economy:

Stimulate the local economy with new sustainable bases
Every feature of this plan reflects a focus on the overall sustainability of the proposed changes. Nowhere is this more important than when planning for the city's economic growth. A city that is founded on an unstable economic base is bound to eventually collapse; therefore, we must carefully consider the elements of economic growth to ensure that the city's future development is spurred by a diverse range of stimuli, reflecting a variety of separate industries.

Goal 1: Capture more of the domestic tourism market by encouraging tourists to stay overnight
One base for future economic growth will come from the expansion of the city's tourism industry. But the city cannot place too much emphasis on this industry. An increase in the tourist trade is only one component of the vision for Edessa's future.

In fact, Edessa already has a significant number of tourists who visit the city each year: some 750,000 visitors.

These visitors generally come to see the waterfalls, staying for only a few hours. Therefore, the city could see a drastic increase in overall tourist spending by simply converting some of these one-day visits into overnight stays.

This can be accomplished through a variety of means, which are covered in much greater detail in the section discussing tourism.

Goal 2: Attract younger residents and create jobs by establishing a university branch
One of the principal goals of the establishment of the new university branch within Edessa is to bring a large

number of young residents to the city. These students will bring a certain level of income to the city and help to support complementary businesses, such as cafes and restaurants near the university buildings.

Furthermore, the university itself will become a major new employer within the city. Beginning with the construction process, an institutional entity like a university can support a large number of workers at all levels of the economy, from support staff to administrators.

Goal 3: Expand the city center by creating an urban waterfront area
The new urban center around the expanded canal and waterfront area will be a unique urban space that will support a significant amount of growth in the city's retail and commercial capacity. The site will host one of the university buildings, and it may also be able to support a modern office typology, with mixed-use commercial areas on the ground level.

Goal 4: Emphasize the city's unique archaeological and ecological attractions
A new focus on those elements which truly make the city unique will be central to the revitalization of Edessa's economy. In this regard, the city must emphasize the unique attractions of its location. In particular, the city should work to support continued excavations of the ancient city, which could help the city capture a larger share of Greek archaeological tourism. Additionally, the proposal included in this plan will situate the city within a diverse network of ecological attractions, including wetlands, hiking, waterfalls, and agri-tourism.

Growth: A vision of the phases for future growth and possible housing typologies

As the city looks to the future and plans for growth in population and city extent, it must consider how and where it can accommodate new development. Although the infrastructure can handle a city of approximately double the current size, there are limits on the available land which would be appropriate for future growth.

One central theme of this plan is that the natural valley between Edessa and Agras must be preserved. Furthermore, the need for adjacent agricultural land for both agri-tourism and for uses associated with the university dictates that much of the flat land to the northwest of the city should remain as a preserved agricultural belt. These limitations dictate many of the subsequent decisions on growth and phasing.

Goal 1: Change the street grid and housing typology in the existing Smareka neighborhood to create higher density
The Smareka neighborhood is the site of the most recent housing developments in Edessa. The neighborhood has several large single-family houses, laid out on a street grid with an extremely large block structure. Luckily, much of the land remains vacant and undeveloped, so it may be possible to alter the trajectory of the area before it is completed.

First, and perhaps most importantly, the city must encourage all future development in this area to take place at a much higher density than it has so far. The surrounding hills with steep slopes mean that the Smareka location is the last flat land adjacent to the city of significant size that may be developed. Therefore it is imperative that the area be developed in a way that makes the most of this opportunity. Because the neighborhood is so close to the expanded canal and urban waterfront area, it seems likely that it will be able to support the higher density of development, even including the low-density housing that has already been built.

But in addition, the street grid must be altered so the blocks are on a more human scale than they are today. The current blocks — which are nearly superblocks — should be divided by building new, smaller roads and footpaths through the blocks, to extend the urban fabric from the rest of the city.

Goal 2: One option: encourage future growth in the nearby villages
Because of the constraints of the natural topography, Edessa's physical expansion will necessarily be limited in

the near future. To preserve the essential character of the existing city, we propose that one option for future growth would be to encourage the further development of the three villages that are in close proximity to Edessa. By shifting the growth to these areas, Edessa becomes the center of a loose network of walkable towns, but it still can retain the feel of a smaller city.

Goal 3: Another option: create a satellite city on the hill to the northwest of the city
After the Smareka neighborhood is more fully developed, the city will once again need to identify land that it can expand to. As already outlined, the preservation of an agricultural belt will push the next round of development farther away from the existing city. Therefore, we propose that the city build a satellite village or node on the hill that lies northwest of the city. The peak of this hill is roughly 1 kilometer from the existing city, which is still within walking distance, so the new village will have a strong connection to the city.

Goal 4: Implement a responsible mix of uses and phasing for the new village
The new village must not be composed of only housing. The satellite village will have a core at the top of the hill containing a small public square and a small amount of retail. This area will hold a neighborhood market and essential local services. The area surrounding this core will be fairly dense, given the slope of the hill, at about 1.0 FAR. The first phase of growth beyond the core will be on the southern slope of the hill, so every house will have access to quality sunlight and views to the valley. This area will be less dense, at roughly 0.5 FAR.

If the city continues to expand and needs more space, it will be possible to develop on the north slope, as well. Because this phase of growth is much more speculative, this area is simply identified as a potential site for future growth. It may be that the needs of the city may change by that time, and another direction for growth may be more appropriate.

Within the neighborhood, we envision a series of a few roads that largely follow the contours of the land, so the roadways are not too steep. The housing would be built in rows with shared walls, because the primary view corridors are to the south.

Because the roadways must follow the topography, the block lengths will be quite large. Therefore, we propose that the blocks should be further broken up by a system of pedestrian paths and stairways that climb the hill toward the core at the crest.

Acknowledgments

The success of the Edessa studio depended on many contributors.

The sponsor of the studio Mayor Ioannis Sontras hosted us for a week during a memorable trip to Edessa. While addressing the studio participants, he inspired us by saying that his local government, when elected, had a choice: "Administer or take action; we chose to take action!"

The vice-mayors and the city council provided us with unprecedented support and were intimately involved in the process. At the final presentation of the students' work in Edessa, we will never forget one of the members who, with tears in his eyes, thanked us for understanding the important role that the now-defunct Agras Waterfalls had played in creating a "heart and soul" of this small community. And that Agras, his community, has been, for more than 50 years, seeking to reinstate the Agras Waterfalls, a clear proposal of our studies. When presented with our plans at the end of the studio, the city council's fears were only that our designs will stay on paper and not be materialized.

Dimitris Metaxas, Efi Ouroumi, and Yannis Vatantzis were among the many employees of the municipality who spent a great deal of time with us, provided information, and responded to the many questions we had. Professor Yannis Tsalikidis, Director of Graduate Studies of Landscape Architecture at the University of Thessaloniki, generously contributed work that his students had previously been done on Edessa, which was tremendously helpful to us. Professor George Mintsis of the Aristotelian University of Thessaloniki advised us on transportation, tourism, and development. Their involvement and presence at the final review at Harvard University is particularly appreciated.

Richard John gave a series of lectures on sustainability and climate change, and spent a week with the studio. Alexios Monopolis gave a series of short lectures on ecology, accompanied us in Edessa, and visited Edessa for a second time to collect information and take photographs. Alexios, with Dimitris Zoupas, who also accompanied us on the trip, developed a case study on sustainability for Edessa. Padraic Kelly of Happold Consulting gave a lecture on water issues and sustainable development. Byron Stigge of Buro Happold advised on engineering issues. Paul Nakazawa advised on business issues.

We would like to thank Mohsen Mostafavi, Charles Waldheim, Felipe Correa, George Liaropoulos-Legendre, Ingeborg Rocker, Scheri Fultineer, Paul Nakazawa, Yannis Tsalikidis, and George Mintsis for their participation in our reviews—a critical learning component of the studio.

Concluding, all of us—students, teaching assistants, and instructors—have felt very close to Edessa and its people. Our connection to Edessa has been reflected in the intensity of our work and our genuine offerings to a sustainable future of Edessa, which exceeded what is expected from a design studio in academia.

We believe this to be a wonderful model for how academia can both serve the pedagogical goals of the university while making a direct contribution to the betterment of our environment. Further, a real emotional connection was made between the students of the GSD, who come from all over the world, and the people of Edessa. We sincerely thank all the people involved for making this studio such a success.

— Professors Martha Schwartz and Spiro N. Pollalis

Abu Dhabi Corniche Beach

As Abu Dhabi continues its transformation from tiny pearling village to diverse global capital city, Martha Schwartz Partners is working with the Abu Dhabi Urban Planning Commission as part of their long-term development strategy for the city's growth. The project asks, "How can we restore Abu Dhabi's emblematic waterfront Corniche as a landmark of the city and as a functional model to take the city sustainably into the future?"

Views of existing beach and Corniche road.

Brief

In every city there are particular spaces that capture the spirit of the place. Central Park in New York, Trafalgar Square in London, and the grand boulevards of Paris—these are the kinds of places that define the identity of a city. In the case of Abu Dhabi, this emblematic space is its 8-kilometer waterfront, which sits on the northern edge of the "North Island" of Abu Dhabi. The Corniche forms the water's edge to the most dense and most built-up part of the city, and given its proximity to the Central Business District, has many sites of cultural significance strung along its distance.

Martha Schwartz Partners is exploring options for the design of the first 4.5 kilometers of the 8-kilometer waterfront promenade and beach that will serve the diverse and growing population of the quickly evolving city. The challenge is to organize the beach and promenade so that it provides multiple options for occupation and flexibility for different situations. An important aspect of this space is that it must function to enable a small native population with a strong cultural heritage to assimilate different immigrant groups into a new, future culture without losing its connections to the past. The new beach and promenade, designed to create manageable spaces of roughly 100 meters, will be heavily programmed with changing rooms, snack bars, restaurants, beach clubs, bike trails, athletics areas, children's play areas, and retail. It must make visual connections back into the city that has been cut off by transit infrastructure. It must handle large festivals and events, while providing places for families to picnic in privacy. It must be a place that is informal and inviting to residents and visitors. It must be a place where children can play safely and adults can dine in elegance. It must be the face of the future for Abu Dhabi.

Left: Site and context. Right: Abu Dhabi Workshop.

Approach

MSP believes that particular sites within the public realm have a responsibility to deliver a design that reflects the aspirations of the city and its citizens. Additionally, it must provide multi-tiered services that deliver an accessible, healthy, and safe environment for people of many cultures and socioeconomic levels so they may enjoy their lives in the city. The public realm is synonymous with "quality of life" for people living in cities. It is a public organ that gives as much to the wealthy as it does to the economically challenged of a city.

The Corniche Beach and Promenade will not only be a model for social health, but ecological health, as well. The approach to the design embraces Estidama, a phrase that means "sustainability" in Arabic. Environmental sustainability has become more critical to the United Arab Emirates as they attempt to transition beyond booming oil-based economies and into functioning, healthy cities that will sustain them into the future. The four pillars of Estidama—environment, economy, society, and culture—are equal to placemaking in guiding MSP's work. Particularly important is whole-life costing, which embeds and invests high quality into the design so that the landscape will last well into the future with as small a carbon footprint as possible.

Context and Considerations

Traffic infrastructure

The site runs parallel to a 6-lane high-speed roadway. This presents a major barrier and cuts off the Corniche Beach and Promenade from the rest of the city. The road, the result of rapid traffic-led planning, is fast, loud, smoggy, and risky to cross. Beach-goers are forced to cross at underpasses or at traffic lights, which occur every 200–300 meters which is a very long distance for the many women who walk to the beach in the heat with small children. Any design for the Corniche Promenade will have to try to ameliorate the many negatives associated with this adjacent high-speed corridor and will have to provide a buffer between the beach and the road.

Existing Open Spaces and City Fabric

The Parks Department is anxious to protect the open spaces that remain on the North Island. There is a desire to keep and develop a strip of space to the south of the Corniche Road as a major recreational destination. As well, the Urban Planning Commission (UPC) and the Parks Department are anxious to include the Corniche Beach and Promenade as part of this open space system

MSP, along with the UPC, has proposed a vision for the Corniche Promenade to provide a continuous public realm zone for pedestrians, bikes, and greenery that would provide a continuous edge that wraps the Mina Zayed Port District and the Central Business District to the east; flows along the entire 8 kilometers of the Corniche Promenade; continues to the Heritage Pier; and with ferries and taxis, connects to the south and north edges of Lulu Island.

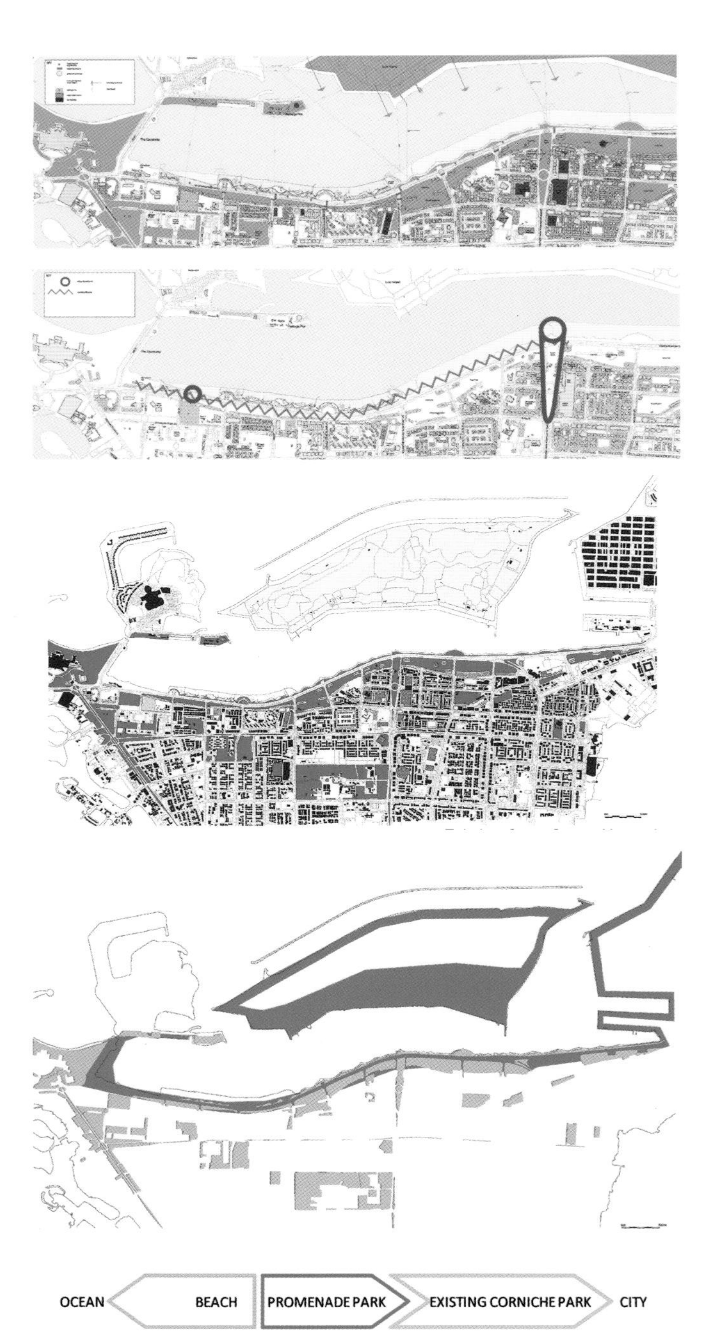

Diagram: The ocean/beach/ Corniche Promenade and Promenade Park is joined to the existing Corniche Park and city. This indicates the desire to modify the present high-speed Corniche Road so these pieces of open space can be reconnected to form a more meaningful series of contiguous spaces.

Top: The Corniche is firmly embedded in the north-south grid of the city's streets, which end at the Corniche Promenade. Although this creates excellent connection to city sidewalks and shade-structure system, the Corniche Road remains a barrier. The dimensions and spacing of the intersections set up an existing rhythm for the placement of retail, as well as suggesting that there must be mid-block signalled pedestrian crossing. The city was clear that they desired to have unobstructed views to the water from these streets.

Bottom:
The Corniche Beach and Promenade sits in a largely residential and dense district of the city. It will service a young population representative of Abu Dhabi.

Program Distribution

Initial evaluation was conducted to examine the distribution of heavily programmed, less programmed, active areas, and passive activities. The active zone to the west was to extend the water activities that might attract the guests of the Hiltonia Hotel, which occupies this end of the Corniche. A vast 2400-meter stretch remains for passive beach activities only. The next 1,500-meter stretch is active, and incorporates sports activities and children's play areas that could be enhanced by activities located in the adjacent park. The last 1,200 meters are more passive and can be a flexible space for cultural events that may happen next to the existing Turaath Cultural Plaza, where the cultural pathway that leads to the historic fort of intersects the Corniche. The plaza also sits at a very important junction of the airport and the Corniche Road.

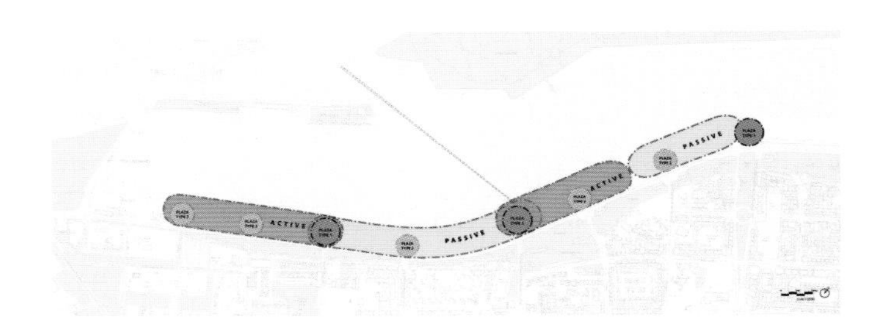

Program Requirements:
2 Ferry Stops
3 Water Taxis
19 Life Guard Stations
8 Cycle Hire Stations
1 Central Office
1 Fine Dining Facility
1 Family Restaurant
1 Beach Club
1 Community Center
1 Cafe
10 Public Amenities (Bathrooms and Changing Rooms)
12 Retail Clusters
1 Outdoor Cinema
8 Fitness Stations
1 Water Sports Center
1 Media Center
1 Beach Sports Center
21 Children's Play Areas
1 Area of Organized Beach Sports

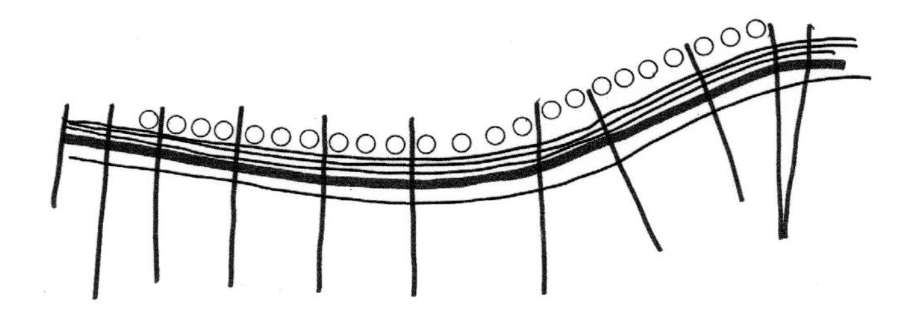

Diagrams exploring possible program distribution across the site.

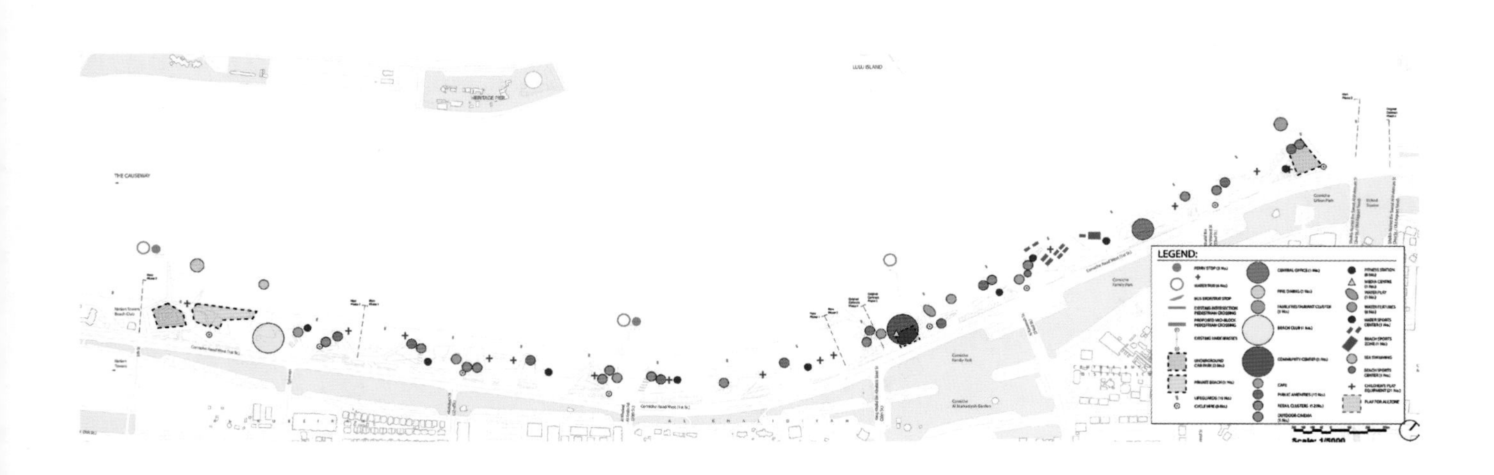

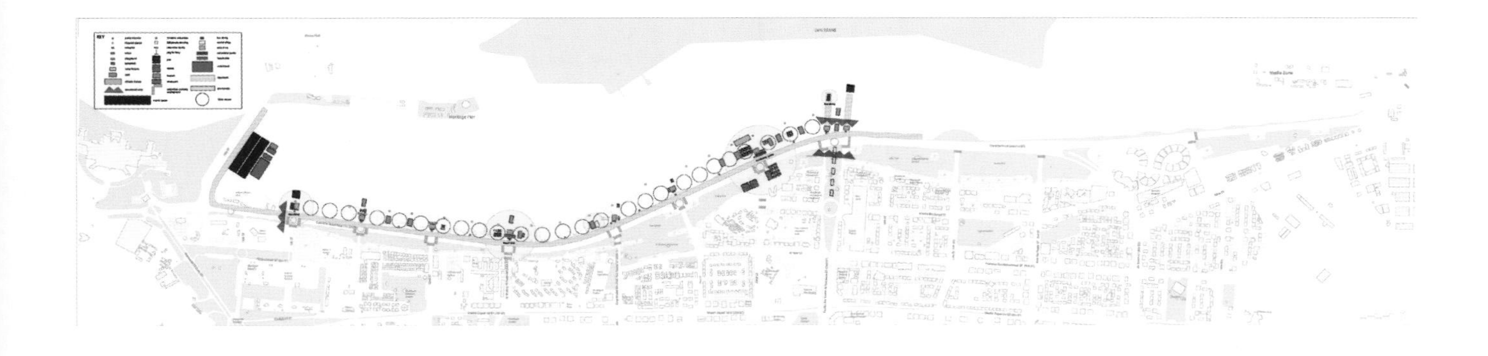

Bottom: This diagram places the uses alongside the 100-meter-diameter “rooms.”

Summary and Objectives

The following items underpinned our goals for what our design should achieve. They would also help to evaluate the design strategies that would come out of the next stage.

From these initial studies and determination of program, our team summarized what we had learned from these exercises. The following items underpinned our goals for what our design should achieve. They would also help to evaluate the design strategies that would come out of the next stage.

Aims

- Innovation – big ideas and vision to ensure a landmark project
- Enhanced Beach Experience – create an edge to the beach that will protect the beach from the intrusion of the road by creating a lifted promenade under which all building program can fit, thereby reducing visual clutter of the beach
- Climate – the Corniche is to be an all-year-round destination
- Comfort – shade is critical
- Culture – respect and respond to cultural sensitivities and diversities
- Heritage – celebrate heritage and culture, including the Turaath Heritage District links, cultural hub, and Heritage Trail
- Neighborhood – the Corniche should link with surrounding neighborhoods
- Water quality – Blue Flag criteria to be attained
- Sustainability – target a three Pearl Estidama rating
- Installation – ensure plans are practical and implementable under local conditions
- Strong Destination – give the new landscape roots in its site and a sense of place

Context

- Dealing with the Corniche road is critical in bridging the city with the waterfront.
- Directly adjacent to a residential area, the new Corniche Beach provides a directly connected neighborhood park with local as well as city-wide significance.
- To register against the strong backdrop of the city, the design of the new Corniche must be equally striking.
- Water is a precious resource and has enormous cultural significance. We need to express care in its use, both seen (fountains or water-play) and unseen (irrigation and cleaning).
- Working in tandem with natural conditions implies a palette of plants adapted to and/or native to the area. See Planting Strategy section.

People

- Carefully incorporate the cultural and social context.
- Engage children to learn through intuition and process. Playful design, spaces, and interactive experiences will be crucial.
- A range of experiences for all ages and abilities should be provided.
- Dedicated facilities for less able-bodied people should be fully integrated and not separated from other landscape elements.
- Design must respond to the many layers of movements and occupations across the site (walkers, cyclists, swimmers, readers, picnickers, etc.)

Views

- Create new views back to the city and the city skyline to key buildings such as Emirates Palace.
- Frame sea views.
- Maintain view corridors from the city to tie the new landscape to its urban context.
- Create new and unexpected views.
- Landform and dense planting should provide a visual barrier from the private beach area to Corniche Road.

Design Language

- Develop an angular theme as the main design concept.
- Incorporate a language of simple elements to provide a coherent whole for a long linear environment.
- Manipulate scale to create a range of experiences, from intimate to open.
- Create an identity by including fine artists and practitioners in the design process.
- Consider and build on the linearity of the site as a unique feature of the paths and routes.
- Wayfinding will be critical to the immediate understanding of the place; and signage, maps, and lettering will be crucial to the branding of the place.
- Planting, hard landscape, and buildings are not

separate entities but are considered and designed together as an integrated landscape.

- Reduce impact of the paraphernalia associated with services, MEP, etc.
- Principal routes connect a sequence of spaces embraced by the landscape and facing the sea, such as outdoor rooms.
- “Furnishing” the rooms with program, planting, and structures lends different character to the spaces.

Climate

- Shade is critical in allowing people to appreciate and use the environment in comfort.
- Vegetation and landform will create a shade corridor and micro-climate for the entire length of the site.
- Evening use will be critical to the success of the site, as most users will want to be there after the heat of the day has passed.
- Landform acts as a wind mitigation measure to prevent sand from blowing into the city.

Systems

- A key consideration is the understanding of all systems (pedestrians, vehicles, bikes, etc.) in parallel (east and west) and perpendicular (north and south) orientations.
- This is a highly prescribed landscape with facilities for many activities. These will be incorporated in a logical and legible manner, and in such a way that the identity of the place as a beach will not be lost.

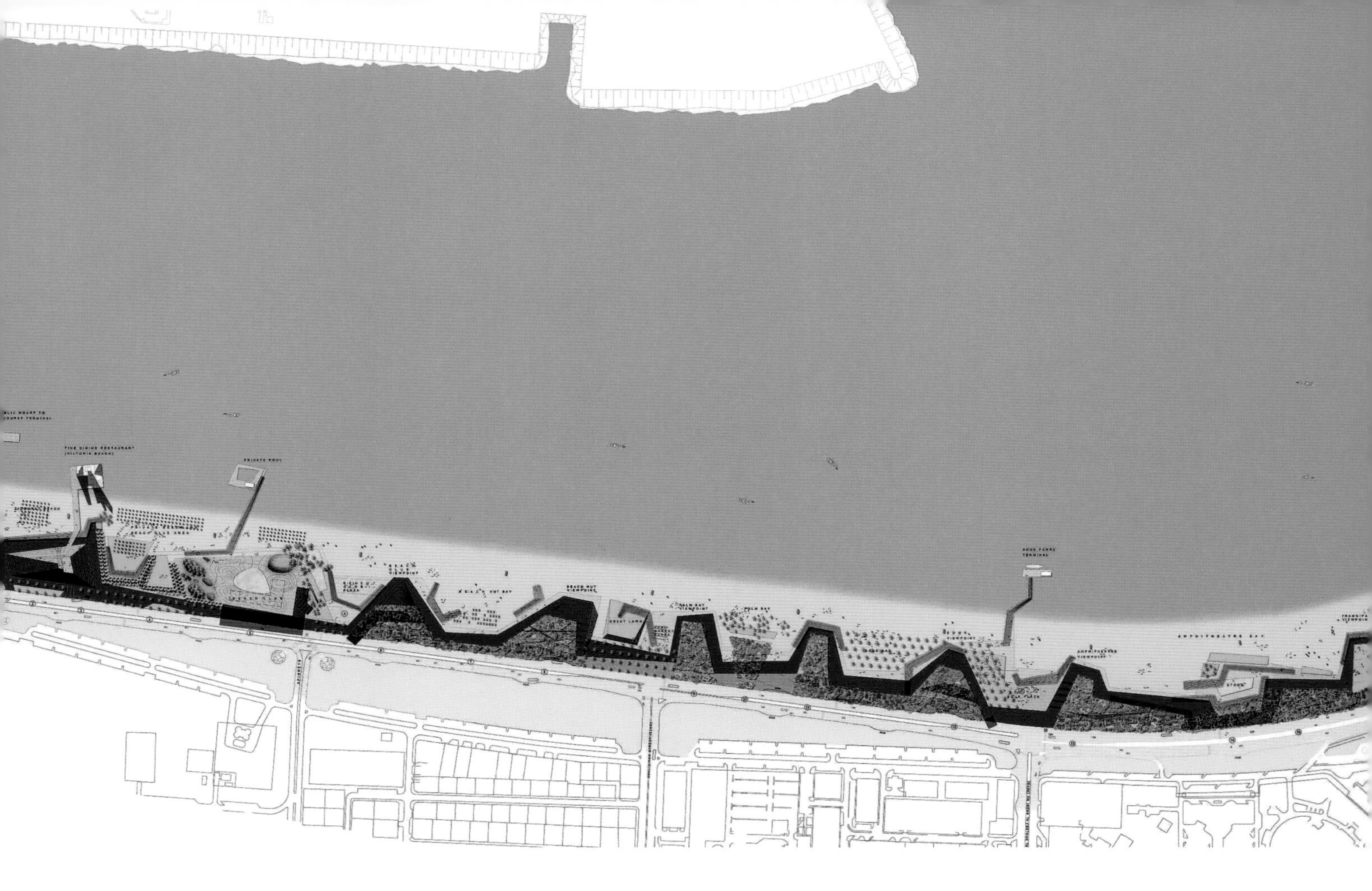

Initial Plan and Direction

Although we are well informed and have a broad set of guidelines and objectives, we now must marry these goals to a physical design that can carry these objectives while creating a visual attraction that will motivate people to visit, use, and stay on Corniche Beach. Given the prominence of this site, the physical expression must be strong, imageable, describable, and coherent enough so that it serves as a symbol for the city of Abu Dhabi.

It is crucial that leadership and end-users be intimately involved in the evolution of the aesthetics, for without people liking what they see, the project will never be able to gain the momentum it will need to see it through to completion. Further, the underlying concept must be robust to endure the many changes, value-engineering exercises, and compromises that public projects are subject to in the normal course of implementation.

The UPC and leadership group worked with MSP to select a scheme that met their objectives and that represented a break from the past. They wished to see something that was new, young, and urban that could represent the "new" Abu Dhabi as it evolves into the future.

We had a number of initial Charrette sketches that expressed this direction, so we applied a couple of them and set them against the long list of objectives that we had devised.

From an iterative process with many stakeholders involved, the "angular scheme" was chosen. The stakeholders wanted something that expressed the urban nature of the city, its grid, and a diversion to the usual flowing forms that have up to now been associated with design in this region. The design was chosen to represent change, youthfulness, and urbanity. The scheme proposes a promenade structure that weaves in and out from the Corniche edge with "fingers" projected out onto the beach. The highly integrated structure contains the entire building program, with change rooms, snackbars, and retail embedded under the raised promenade. The idea is to create a simple, adaptable structure that can evolve as the city grows and changes.

The fingers create different "covers" along the beach in response to the anticipated variety of users and uses for the beach. Each cove will be programmed differently;

some will be plazas with dense retails, others will be children's play areas, and others will be filled with palms for quiet reading in the shade. The top of the jutting finger forms will be a smooth, grass surface to support and encourage the active picnicking culture in the city. Three long piers reach out into the water and house programs such as water taxis, ferry docks, restaurants, a deep-water swimming area, and a beach club.

Over the coming months, these schemes will be formalized and tested against the site parameters and program.

Corniche promenade and beach masterplan, not to scale.

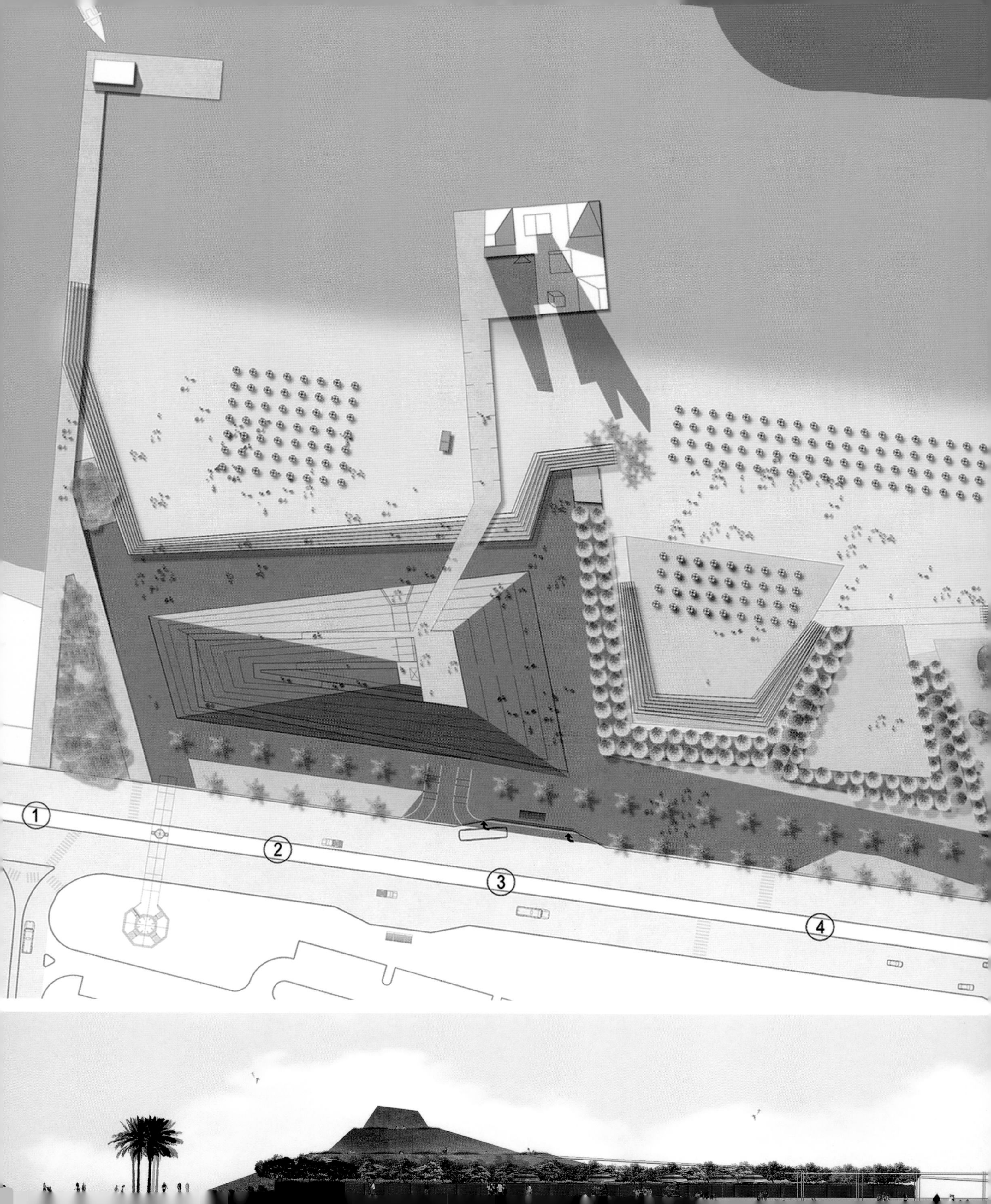
1
2
3
4

Ziggurat plan and section, not to scale.

"The Corniche Beach and Promenade will not only be a model for social health, but ecological health, as well. The approach to the design embraces *Estidama*, a phrase that means 'sustainability' in Arabic."

Top: View of planted promenade. Bottom: View of play area at night.

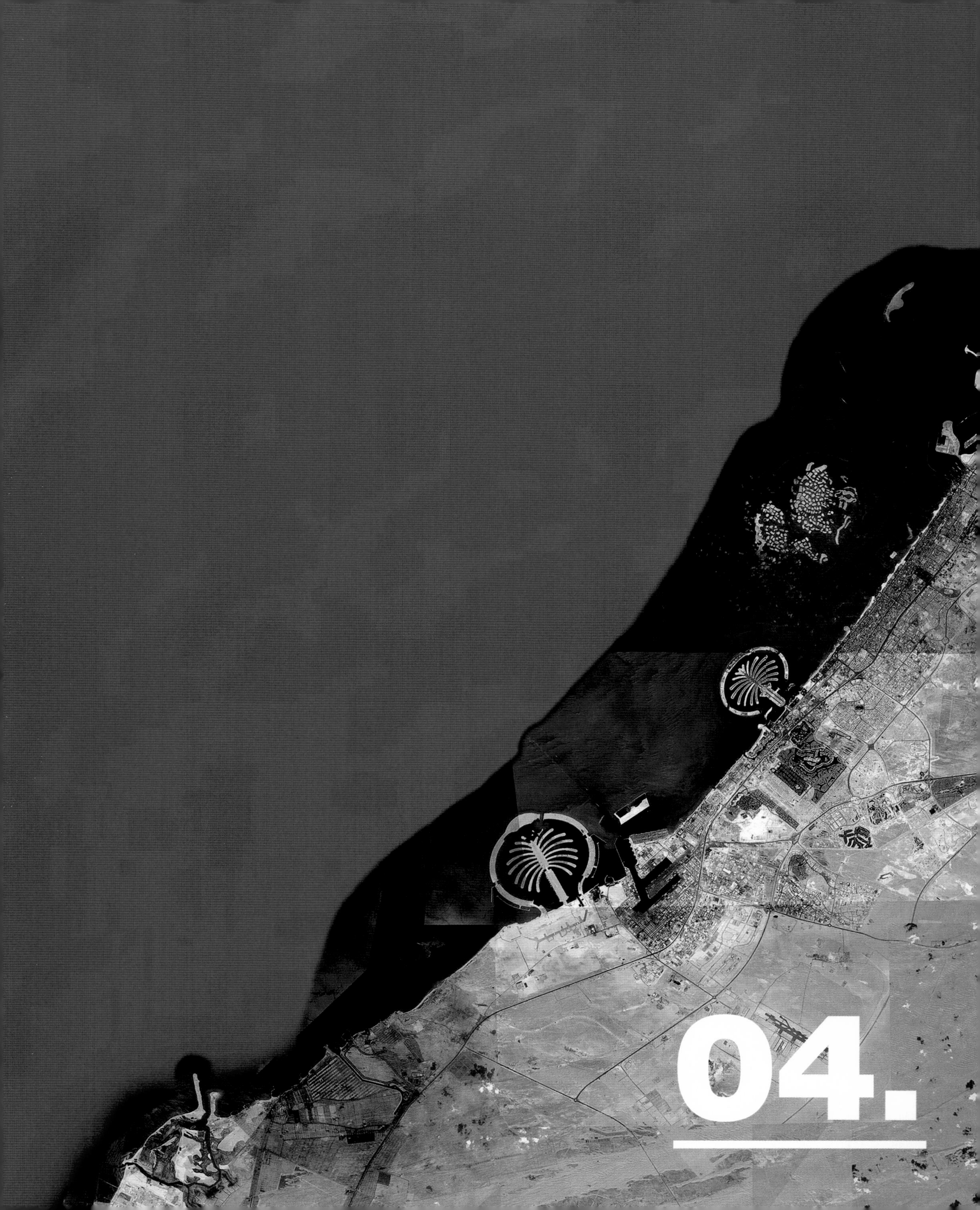

04.

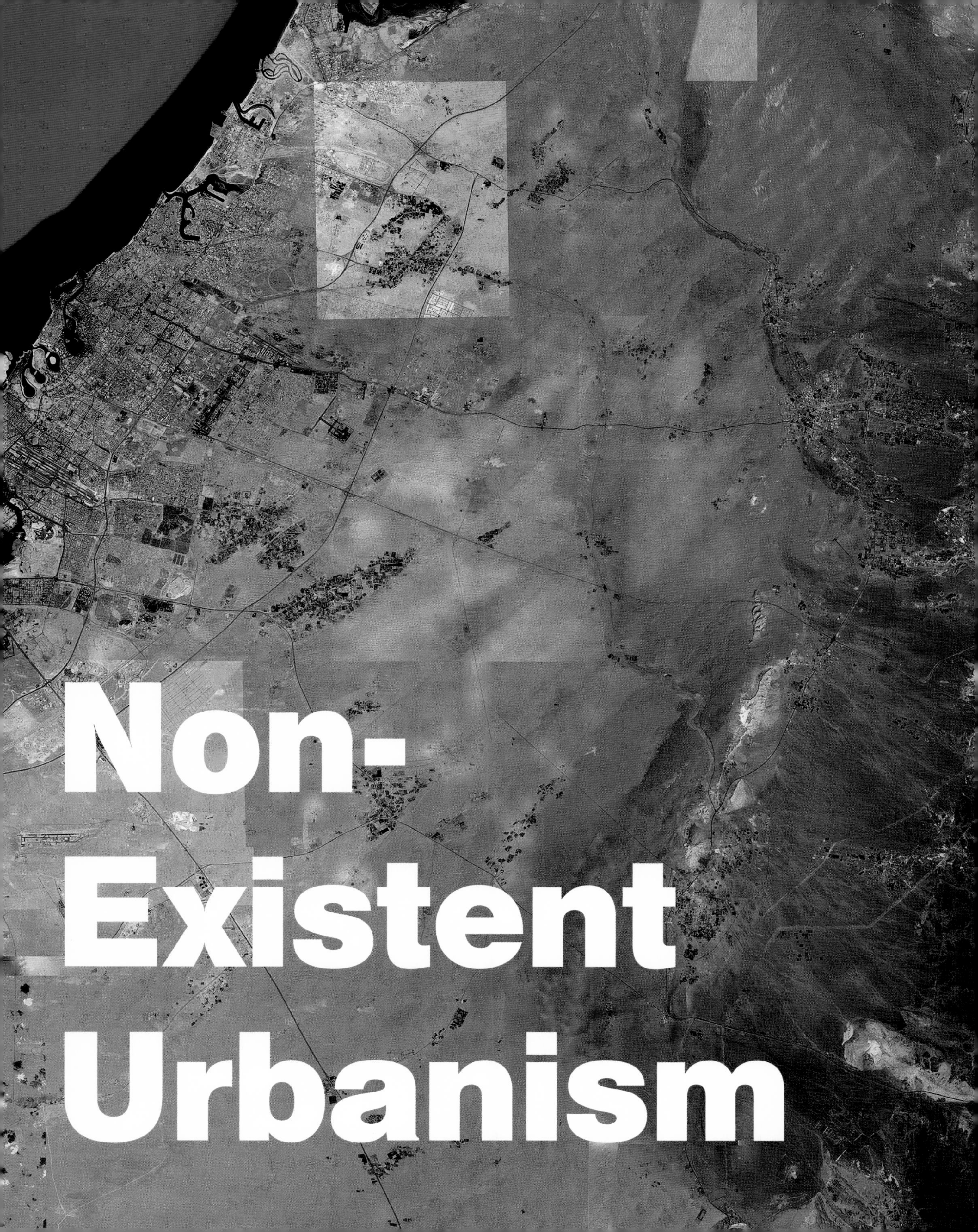
Non-
Existent
Urbanism

Recent "from-scratch" cities and rapid suburban sprawl raise questions about how to activate vital cities where there is no existing population density, no urban context, and no discernible center. In these cases, urban activity must be generated. Destinations must be created, identities forged, and the sense of place intensified to introduce urban life where it previously did not exist.

From left: Mesa Arts Center, Mesa, Arizona; Jumeirah Gardens, Dubai, UAE

Jumeirah Gardens

In a period of less than 40 years, Dubai has grown from a nearly barren desert to a city with a skyline to rival New York's. This rapid growth has had an intense impact on the city's infrastructure, population, and ecological health, leaving little choice but to forge a new direction of growth for the future. Working within a master plan prepared by SOM, Martha Schwartz Partners has designed a conceptual framework for the central park of Dubai's Jumeirah Garden City, a new development representing a sustainable approach to the expanding city.

Views of Jumeirah Gardens within context of the proposed Jumeirah Garden City.

City Within a City

Conceived as a "city within a city," the new mixed-use neighborhood will accommodate a population of 680,000 people, including 270,000 residents, 410,000 office workers, and 40,000 daily commuters. The new neighborhood establishes crucial links between Dubai's central city and its ever-evolving waterfront. The area is divided into seven distinct districts and is organized around a 50-acre central park that will provide the public recreational space for the new residents.

Emphasizing sustainable principles, accessible transit, and an active public realm, the project reinforces Dubai's image as a site of influential architecture and global business while representing its new direction toward a balanced and sustainable future.

Sustainability Targets:
- Improve 35% energy efficiency
- Improve 40% water efficiency
- Condense water cooling for district cooling by seawater
- 90% wastewater reuse
- Large central park and landscaping to reduce heat island effect
- 45% reduction in domestic waste
- 80% demolition and excavation waste diverted from landfill
- Indoor environment quality will be improved
- Improved walkability

Aerial view of East Park.

Background and Approach

Dubai did not have time to grow sustainably. In a 35-year period beginning in 1970, its population grew more than 20 times to a total of over 1.2 million by 2005. This population, including the more than 500,000 laborers who came in to build the new city, placed incredible pressure on the city's solitary sewage treatment plant and the single desalinization plant where the city gets its fresh water. Dubai's skyline, which appeared nearly as quickly as its population, is composed of hundreds of towers. Each one stands as a solitary "island" with little connection to the ground plane or the other surrounding buildings, leaving no public realm connection in the city. The area that could have been a pedestrian zone has now been eclipsed by the ever-expanding main thoroughfare, Sheik Zayed Road, which has become more and more congested as more cars are added to the city daily.

Both SOM and MSP see Jumeirah Gardens as an opportunity to address some of the imbalances caused by Dubai's rapid growth and as a chance to provide Dubai with a vital public space to meet the complex needs of this complex city.

From left: Aerial view of Dubai growth; Traffic on Sheik Zayed Road; Jumeirah Garden City masterplan, not to scale.

Analysis and Observations

Population

- From 1985–2008 Dubai's population grew from 370,000 to 1.3 million.
- Only 17% of Dubai's population are native Emirates.
- 85% of the non-native population are South Asian laborers from India, Pakistan, and Bangladesh.
- The ratio of men to women in Dubai is 3:1

Public Realm and Connectivity

- Dubai has more buildings taller than 200 meters than any city in the world.
- Buildings are isolated and without connection.
- There is limited possibility for walking and cycling.
- There is no public realm connectivity at street grade.

Water Supply

- The Emirates desalinate the equivalent of four billion bottles of water a day.
- At any given time, the region has, on average, an estimated four-day supply of fresh water.
- The desalinization plant process is raising salinity levels in the ocean, threatening local flora and fauna.

Sewage Treatment

- Dubai's sole sewage treatment plant cannot keep up with the rapid growth.
- Wastewater from 1.3 million residents is trucked to the treatment plant. Much of this is illegally disposed.
- Raw sewage in the ocean has forced beaches in the area to close.

Overview of park looking toward mosque.

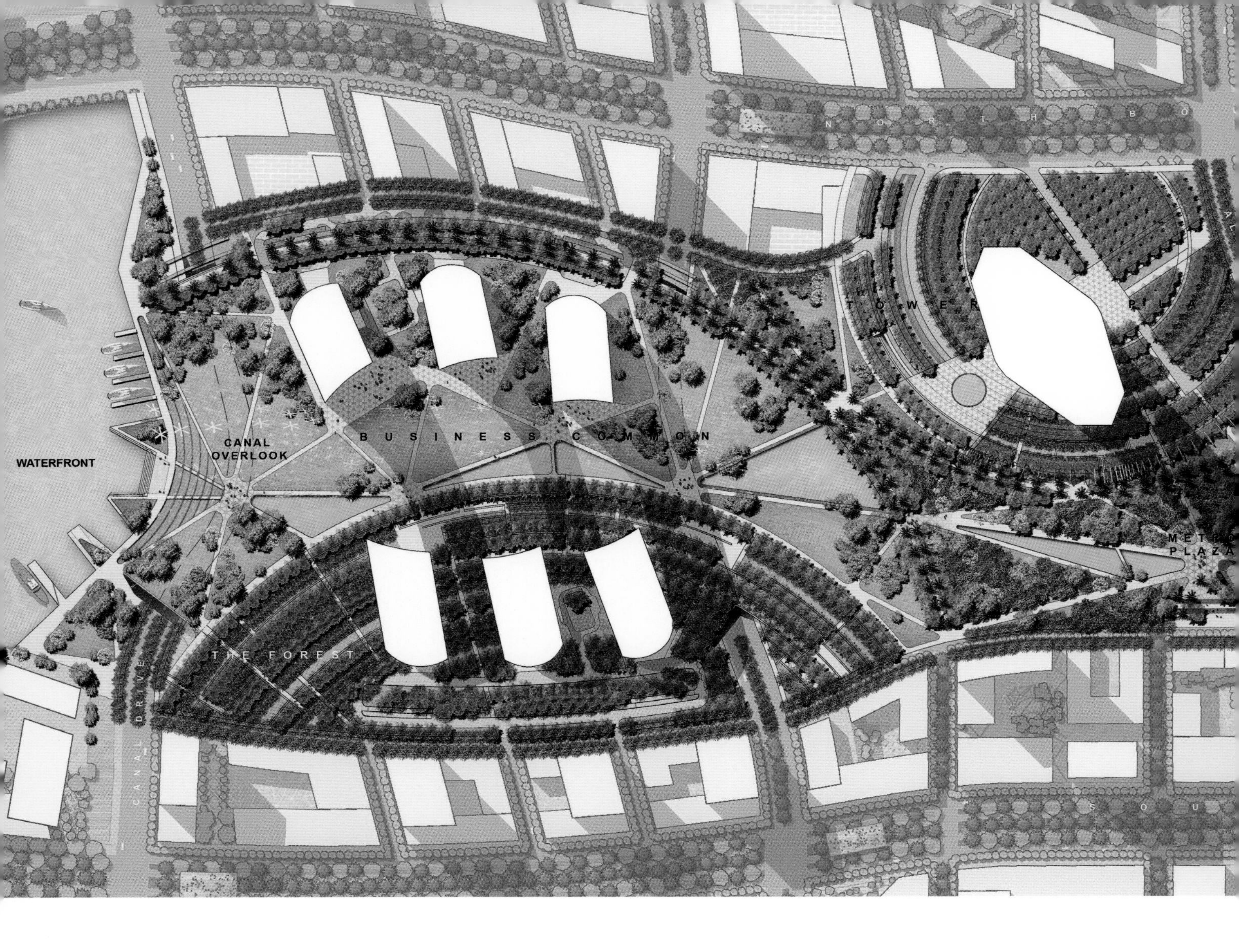
WATERFRONT
CANAL
OVERLOOK
BUSINESS COMMON
THE FOREST
CANAL DRIVE
PLAZA

Connection to the Neighborhood

To avoid the “island” effect that is seen around so many of the towers in Dubai, MSP uses the edges of the park to stitch the seven districts of the new city together. Around the edges of Jumeirah Gardens, giant crescent gardens reach out into the surrounding neighborhood to invite people into the park. Each garden relates to a specific district of the new city, acting as a smaller neighborhood park for local residents. The crescent gardens lead visitors from the quiet edge of the park toward the vibrant central spine that holds the more civic programs of the park, including a mosque, an amphitheater, and the business common.

Site plan, not to scale.

A Park for the People

One of the main challenges for Jumeirah Gardens is to serve the extremely diverse population who will be moving into the new neighborhood. As it is in the rest of Dubai, this population is expected to be a mix of Emirates, Americans, Europeans, Australians, and Asians—many different cultures each with its own traditions of parks and its own culture of engaging with open spaces. The park will be the meeting point for this diverse range of people and must provide opportunities for integration, but also for isolation.

To accommodate these different needs, MSP provides one large space in the center of the park for larger, more active gatherings and a series of smaller, more intimate "rooms" distributed through the crescents along the edge of the park. The rooms are more densely planted, offering enclosure and privacy while still maintaining a visual connection to the central civic space. The different zones of the park offer a flexible structure to allow the open space to transition with Dubai as it continues to grow and change into the future.

View of one of the garden 'rooms' along the edge of the park.

Harnessing Local Resources

Working in conjunction with SOM's master plan and with Dubai's vision for the future, MSP's vision for Jumeirah Gardens includes many sustainable practices. As fresh water is extremely scarce in the United Arab Emirates, MSP takes advantage of the population density of the new neighborhood, proposing to irrigate the park and supply its water features exclusively with recycled greywater from the nearby buildings. The water recycling strategy will serve to relieve pressure on the city's overburdened sewage treatment plant. The scheme also takes advantage of the building heights of the new neighborhood, using passive cooling techniques to pull cooler air from above the buildings to cool pedestrians passing by at street level. MSP is also exploring options for connecting the business district with the new transit system underground and semi-underground corridors through the park. By providing expedient and shaded routes to and from the transit hub, the corridors will make transit a more desirable option for Dubai residents.

The project represents a necessary shift in Dubai's previously unbridled growth patterns and offers an example of some of the advantages of working with "from-scratch" urban conditions. New buildings and new development, unencumbered by existing infrastructure, offer opportunities for sustainable approaches including innovative water recycling, alternative energy sources, and new materials.

The park's water features and irrigation will be fed by greywater from the surrounding buildings.

View of central sport fields and active recreation zone.

Mesa Arts Center

By population, Mesa is larger than St. Louis, Miami, and Cleveland. All of the people who live in the city center, however, could sleep one to a room at the new Cosmopolitan Hotel in Las Vegas. Mesa Arts Center is positioned to turn the sprawling city back inward to build a downtown where there has never been one before.

Top: Aerial view of Mesa Arts Center. Bottom: View down 'arroyo' toward the Arts Center buildings.

Mesa's 1-square-mile historic downtown has retained the same dimensions since it was established in 1874. As the city's population began to grow steadily, nearly doubling every decade from the 1940s through the 1990s, it did not add density to the existing downtown, but instead spread out into the surrounding desert. The city now sprawls across a 134-square-mile area.

Mesa's exponential population growth mirrors that of neighboring Phoenix, just a half hour's drive down the freeway. As Phoenix grew as a city, Mesa grew as a bedroom community. Both populations rose steadily during the Second World War as several major defense contracts awarded to local manufacturing companies demanded labor. After the war, the area continued to attract manufacturing industries and, in particular, electronics. This led naturally to a rapid explosion in the 1970s and 1980s with the rise of the high-tech industries that continue to cluster in the Valley today. Major industries, small companies, young singles, and retirees continue to flock to the area, attracted by its pro-growth philosophy, its relatively low living costs, and its famously friendly climate—warm winters and more than 300 sunshine days per year.

Aerial view of Mesa's typical low, sprawling development.

Although the Phoenix metropolitan area, composed of Scottsdale, Tempe, and Mesa, is now the 14th largest metropolitan area in the United States, it feels anything but urban. This city grew up in the automobile age. Characterized by low-density sprawl, limited transit options, and impressive freeway infrastructure, the area's suburban growth pattern has made it impossible for Mesa to maintain a vibrant city-center.

By the mid 1990s, Mesa's historic downtown had been eclipsed by its sprawling periphery. There was no identity or destination left in the downtown square mile, just a quiet corridor of wide streets, empty stores, and fast food chains. The city, known for its lack of residential property taxes, didn't have the revenue stream to invest in revitalizing its city-center, and there was not a large enough downtown population to support the local retail and restaurants. Those who did live nearby went to the newer, larger, suburban shopping centers for food, shopping, and entertainment. Downtown Mesa was not an attractive environment for new businesses.

But the city wanted to change that. They wanted to reinvent (or invent for the first time) Mesa's downtown—they wanted to put Mesa on the map. In 1994 a community group, the Mesa Arts Alliance, began exploring ideas for a visual and performing arts center that they hoped would catalyze development and density in the downtown core. In order to generate enough energy to recast the image of sleepy, suburban Mesa, they would need to create a powerful identity and an unmistakable destination in the downtown core.

This destination would be the Mesa Arts Center complex, designed by Boora Architects and Martha Schwartz Partners. The MAC, with its three theaters, five galleries, a school for the arts, public space, and an active program of education and events, was positioned to generate enough momentum to begin the transformation of downtown Mesa.

Left: Historic postcard of Main street, Mesa. Right: Main street entrance to the Arts Center landscape.

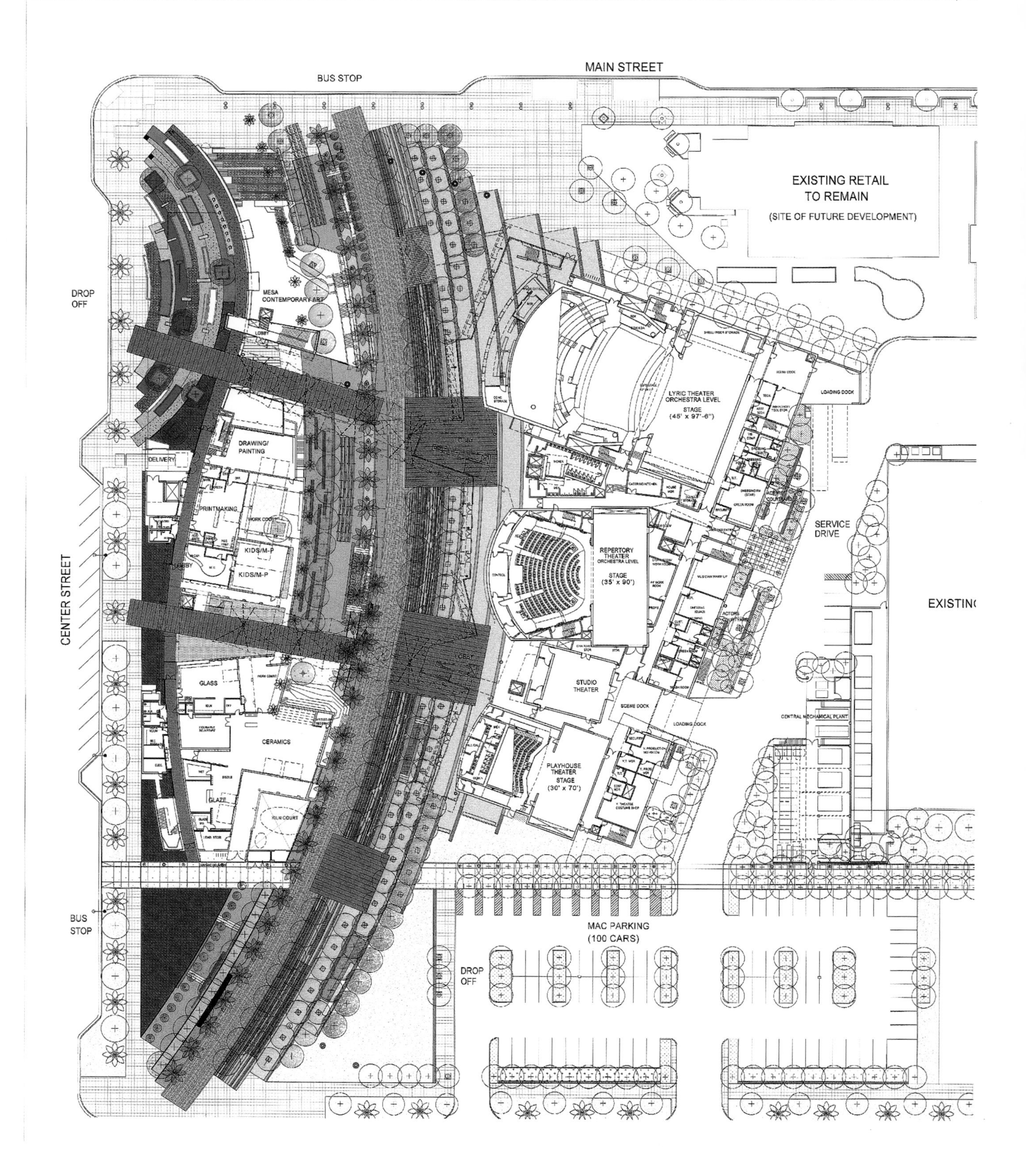

MAIN STREET
BUS STOP
EXISTING RETAIL
TO REMAIN
(SITE OF FUTURE DEVELOPMENT)
DROP
OFF
MESA
CONTEMPORARY ART
LYRIC THEATER
ORCHESTRA LEVEL
STAGE
(45' x 97'-6")
LOADING DOCK
DRAWING/
PAINTING
DELIVERY
PRINTMAKING
KIDS/M-P
KIDS/M-P
REPERTORY
THEATER
ORCHESTRA LEVEL
STAGE
(35' x 90')
SERVICE
DRIVE
EXISTIN
CENTER STREET
STUDIO
THEATER
SCENE DOCK
LOADING DOCK
GLASS
CERAMICS
CENTRAL MECHANICAL PLANT
PLAYHOUSE
THEATER
STAGE
(30' x 70')
GLAZE
KILN COURT
BUS
STOP
MAC PARKING
(100 CARS)
DROP
OFF

Active Street Edge

The intersection of Main and Center streets, the new home of the MAC, was right at the heart of downtown Mesa, but there was no downtown to be found. The 100-foot-wide streets, indicative of the city's Mormon roots, were made big enough to accommodate a U-turn with a team of oxen[1] and are lined with low, one-story shops and massive surface parking lots, leaving no discernible street edge or urban fabric.

When Boora Architects, led by Bud Oringdulph and Martha Schwartz Partners, designed the master plan for the 8-acre site, they knew they needed to create an active street edge to provide a new density along the otherwise vacant street edge. In order to accomplish this, the designers sited the academic building program with a direct relationship to Center Street. "We felt that having a plan with a big open space against the street was like bringing coals to Newcastle. What they really needed was a street edge to reinforce the fabric of the city."

Left: Site plan, not to scale. Right: The Arts Center landscape and buildings frame a street edge along Mesa's wide downtown streets.

These outer buildings create the much-needed street edge on one side, and a large, arc-shaped interior space on the other. This interior offers a rich public space in, around, and on top of the five gallery spaces and three theaters. The public space, designed by MSP, gives an address to the MAC and lends a visible sense of change and excitement to the previously quiet downtown core.

To generate activity along the dormant downtown streets, the new one-block complex needed to create a dynamic relationship with the adjacent intersection. People are pulled into the center of the site by a giant arced walkway—the "Shadow Walk"—that reaches out to both corners on the new Center Street edge. The route is curved so pedestrians cannot see the whole way into the site, unless they continue on through the block to satisfy their curiosity. Once inside, they will find that the entire block has been transformed into a giant urban stage brought to life by performance, where every surface, every tree, every building, and every visitor is part of the show.

Left: Detail view of shadow walk. Right: View of Arroyo.

Source of Movement from the Local Landscape

The Shadow Walk itself is animated by Mesa's hallmark resource: the sun. Anyone who has been to the Southwest can tell you that there are no crisper shadows anywhere in the country. Long curving rows of trees and shade canopies throw sharp shadows against the walkway, creating a constantly changing surface for visitors to explore. Rows of varying species of local cacti planted against different-colored glass panels are backlit by the afternoon sun, performing a daily shadow play for passersby. The yellow, red, and blue panels have become a popular stage for visitors who perform their own shadow plays for their friends and families.

Another famous Mesa landscape feature adds a different kind of movement to the site. The "Arroyo," which runs the entire length of the Shadow Walk, draws its cyclical flow from the dramatic fluctuation of regional water levels. Mesa is primarily an arid desert landscape except for when it is inundated with flash floods that scour quickly and aggressively across the hard, dry land. The Arroyo,

patterned after the area's expectant river washes, is a dry, boulder-filled riverbed that people can occupy and explore until a concrete basin at one end of the site fills up with water and releases it in a violent crash, filling the entire riverbed up to the brim. The water slowly releases and makes its way back to the concrete basin, where it begins the cycle again. This beloved feature has become an indelible character in Mesa's memory as the backdrop to countless family Christmas cards and wedding photos that are shot here each year.

Left: Cactuses perform shadow plays in the sun. Right: The bubbling arroyo (shown here full and empty) reflects the water cycles of the Mesa desert landscape.

"We had more dreams and aspirations than we had money, so we had only one shot at making a community's dreams come true. We had an aging, tired, boring, dead downtown that we wanted to rejuvenate, and we had a plethora of local arts groups—really good ones—that desperately needed a venue in which to thrive and grow. We were determined to create a downtown urban space that would do something no one else had yet done: combine arts education, visual arts, performing arts, and an urban park space in an environment so collaborative, so beautiful, and so impressive that people visiting our Mesa Arts Center would look at it and say, 'WOW! What city are we in? Surely, this couldn't be dull and boring Mesa, Arizona!'

It has worked in that way and there have been some unexpected results. too. It has become a very popular place for people to go to have their family photos taken and for brides to have their wedding photos done. It was listed a few months ago in the Arizona Republic as one of the top five venues in the Valley to have your family pictures taken. That was unexpected. Many of the charter schools in the area choose to do their graduation ceremonies at the MAC. We never could have anticipated that, either.

It is definitely a place that you would bring visitors when they came from out of town. The Arts Center is a point of pride. It's beautiful. You have this typical 1960s-looking downtown and then you come into the intersection, and there's this arts center covering this whole city block, and it's magnificent."

— Joannie Flatt, former President, Mesa Arts Alliance

Emergency

Actors and Animators

In addition to the dramatic flux offered by regional landscape features, the Arts Center is animated by the performance of people as they move through the site. The sloped grass plane along the Shadow Walk provides the perfect place to sit and watch people go by while the steps of the school offer amphitheater seating for informal and programmed events. The communal "water table" invites community gathering, and areas outside the theater fill up with people talking about the show they have just seen inside.

The generous proportions and variety of informal stages allow the entire Arts Center landscape to be heavily programmed throughout the year, changing it quickly from a breakdancing stage, to a jazz club, to a high school graduation venue. No matter what, it is always busy at the MAC.

The entire landscape is designed as a stage to host concerts and live performances.

The Image of Mesa

Since the Arts Center was built, there has been near-constant activity on the site. It has become a busy destination for both Mesa residents and out-of-town visitors and is the iconic image of Mesa. Although the rest of downtown has yet to catch up with the success of the Arts Center, the city continues to draw energy from the momentum of the MAC, and the identity of downtown is forever associated with the vibrant, buzzing energy of the center and its dynamic landscape.

The Arts Center has become the number one location in Mesa to have family portraits and wedding photos taken.

OLD NAVY

The Softer Side of Sustainability

Martha Schwartz

Beyond Green Roofs

In recent sustainability discussions, there has been altogether too much talk focused on buildings. Planners, architects, and city leaders have often been slow to recognize the important role played by the broader landscape underlying our cities' buildings. The spaces between buildings that Jan Gehl speaks about desperately need to be considered if we are to create sustainable and healthy cities.

However, the focus on buildings is understandable, as the sheer intensity of resources and energy used in construction and operations of buildings overshadows the less resource-hungry landscape by far. In addition with technical guidelines, LEED ratings, and the myriad technological solutions available to architecture, it is easy to understand (and quantify) its place within sustainable practice. Without a technological imperative for dealing with climate change, landscape architects have been relegated to providing green roofs for buildings—basically, a technical section. On a project-by-project basis, our scope is generally small and focuses on the technical performance of the ground plane. The lack of a clear voice for the landscape architect in this discussion is both ironic and problematic, as the landscape is the actual "green" part of the "green" discussion.

However, times are changing quickly. New mega-cities, a vast global trend towards urbanization, and a world population of 7 billion cast the urban landscape in a whole new light, forcing us to reassess its role in sustainable city building. The awareness of landscape as a built piece of infrastructure is crucial to a city's performance and liveability, but this is a new paradigm and one that is little appreciated by most planners and city builders. We need to project an understanding of the urban landscape as more than the leftover spaces between buildings—as its own distinct organ within the city that must be respected, funded, planned, and designed. Collectively, the public realm landscape can provide and enable a positive life for the people who live in cities. The urban landscape must be understood as a piece of a city's infrastructure—the same way we would view our sewers, power, IT connections, and transportation—and as an integrated and necessary urban element that serves a plethora of needs, including places for citizens to meet, recreate, and connect to one another, while serving the natural environment.

Expanded Scope Of Sustainability

So, where does landscape architecture fit at the "Roundtable of Sustainability"? What is our role as professionals, if not to do green roofs and atria for "green" buildings? The answer to this rests in urban and regional scaled interventions. While dealing on a site-by-site basis is how most of us practice, the ability to impact issues of climate change and population growth must occur at the urban scale. It is within the expanded scope of sustainability—one that includes social, political, economic, and ecological performance—that our role as landscape architects resides.

"Soft" Systems

Along with the more environmental technical role the urban landscape performs, the public realm landscape is shaped by other human-generated "soft" systems: the social, cultural, economic, and political operations of people and communities. These "soft systems" play a large role in making a community or city liveable, and are not rooted in technology, but in the physical, psychological, and emotional operations of our own, very human behaviour. I have observed that these "soft" systems are often not given proper recognition or priority in planning and designing communities and cities. However, without their inclusion in the planning and design process, it will be impossible to design successful public spaces, or to achieve sustainability, not only on a city scale, but at any scale.

I consider these "soft" systems to be the most important domain of the landscape architects when working within the urban landscape. In order to create a more sustainable future, we must understand that as landscape architects, our professional remit is firmly embedded in humanism as well as ecology.

The Urban Landscape and Health

The public realm landscape underwrites both environmental and human health by providing access to public transportation, bike lanes, and well-maintained and safe sidewalks. Jan Gehl has a great deal of evidence for how bicycling not only helps the environment by cutting down carbon pollution, but also keeps people more fit, which decreases the cost of public health services dramatically. Urban parks and open spaces provide opportunities for recreation, sports, running, jogging, and walking within dense urban environments that otherwise do not support these activities. In places like the United States, where more than 300,000 people die each year from inactive lifestyle-related causes, the benefits of access to free and accessible recreation space cannot be underscored enough.

The environmental benefits of the urban landscape are well documented and discussed. Parks and open spaces serve to facilitate water percolation, reduce run-off, allow for trees to produce oxygen, create shade and reduce heat load, provide erosion and flood control, provide habitat for flora and fauna, capture particulates in the air, and assist in reducing pollution.

The Urban Landscape and the Economy

The public realm can help to underwrite an urban economy by making sure that places of business are easily accessible, well connected, and served by lively streets and open spaces. Local businesses need to be incorporated into the planning of public realm improvements. The mayors of major cities (such as London's former mayor, Ken Livingstone, Mayor Bloomberg of New York, Mayor Daley of Chicago, and leaders of cities such as San Francisco, Vancouver, and Copenhagen) acknowledge the role that the public realm landscape plays in keeping existing population and by attracting new populations to their cities so they can grow their economies and thrive.

Sophisticated mayors now consider well-educated people to be "capital" and "resources." Without an educated population, the economies of these cities cannot compete and thrive. This is especially important against the backdrop of the decreasing population in Europe. The beautification of a city and the accessibility to green spaces and tree-lined streets are used to entice knowledge-based workers to come to live and work in that city. People have choices and will choose cities that can offer them the highest quality of life.

The Proximity Principle and Quantifying Value of Urban Parks

Understanding the monetary value of the public realm is extremely important in the discussion of investment in parks and open spaces. Fortunately, there is more and more research being produced on this topic, with hard evidence of how well-designed public parks add to the economic proposition of an entire city.

The proximity principle suggests that the value of living near a park is captured in the price of the surrounding properties. This is not a new concept. Upon the construction of Central Park, Olmsted tracked the adjacent property values of buildings near the park to show that their property taxes alone would pay for the construction of the park. In the 17 years following the park's construction, the property values in the area were 16 times greater than the initial cost of the park. Current studies of Central Park continue to support Olmsted's initial instincts about the value of the park. Central Park is currently valued at $627 million an acre or 26% more than the entire 2006 U.S defense budget, and it has been shown that the net value of Manhattan would be less if Central Park was developed. (Sarah Nicholls Parks & Recreation Study, March 2004)

Chicago's Millennium Park, completed in 2004, also had an extensive study conducted on its economic impact, undertaken by Goodman Williams Group and the URS Group. Some excerpts from their findings are remarkable:

- The park attracted an inward migration back to the city by attracting 20,000 new people to downtown.
- The total value of Residential Development attributable to Millennium Park: $1.4 billion.
- Total visitor spending over the next ten years from 2005 to 2015 will range between $1.9 billion and $2.6 billion

DeVries estimates that Millenium Park:

- Increased hotel earnings annually by $42–58 million a year
- Increased restaurant earnings by $67– 87 million

These studies, and many others like them, show how the value of public realm organs within a city stands in stark contrast to the architecture-led development of places like Dubai. A great experiment of the "naughts," Dubai demonstrated clearly that buildings alone do not make a city. The character of a city comes through good planning; the quality of the housing stock; and the design of attractive streets and pedestrian walkways, parks, and open spaces. These are the elements that create a city's character—much more so than individual signature buildings. The specifics of the architecture make little difference to the overall image of a city. We all choose to live in a neighborhood first before we choose the house.

The Public Realm Landscape and Politics

The public realm landscape must serve a political agenda, as the will of the greater public is expressed in the public services and spaces needed for people to work and live. The offer of parks, recreational activities,

"If I could go back and recreate London, I would preserve green corridors coming into the city from the surrounding countryside to provide uninterrupted swathes of green and to allow everyone close access to real bits of nature instead of manicured lawns."

—Ken Livingstone, former Mayor of London

"If we spend more time on the streets, the city will be more lively. If there are more people, more density, and a good mixture of uses, it will be a safer city. The city will work as a better meeting place, because you meet your fellow citizens naturally. At the moment, we are more and more dispersed, living in bigger flats and more privatized spaces, and the public side of life is fading. You cannot find a single city that doesn't wish to make the city center more vibrant or more lively."

— Jan Gehl, Principal, Gehl Architects, Copenhagen

beauty, and quality of life reflect the demands of a city's citizens. If the design and planning of these elements are not done in such a way that the citizens and stakeholders are included in the process, then the outcome may not be valued and maintained over time, nor serve a sustainable goal. Also, given the public nature of this territory, the political landscape must be understood in order to get enough support for a project to make it happen. Not understanding this territory is one of the major reasons that some projects fail.

The Public Realm Landscape and Social Health

Especially important for new, growing, and densifying cities, the public realm landscape provides the arena for social interaction and integration of immigrant communities. The process by which new cultures evolve from older ones happens in cities. It is here in the cities' parks, sports fields, and plazas where people from different backgrounds meet and eventually forge new cultures, a necessity for growth and social evolution. Social integration is a hallmark of cities that remain relevant, attractive, politically stable, and economically and culturally active. In cities, people of different backgrounds and cultures influence one another as they incorporate progressive lifestyle changes into the fabric of their diverse daily lives. The public realm is the "pot" in which the melting happens. This cannot happen in one's living room.

Cultural Life and the Landscape

The ability for the public realm landscape of a city to provide the forum for the cultural life of a city is now of utmost importance, as the cultural and environmental health of cities is at the top of a mayor's "to do" list to maintain a vibrant urban population. The cultural offer of a city is a huge attractor and is itself a new industry. Activities that were once found only inside museums and theaters are now in the streets and spaces of cities, where one can enjoy street performance, concerts, art installation, and dance. The public realm landscape is the new stage for cultural events. Such openness and generosity reflect a lively and open city where people from all parts of the globe can participate, integrate, and enjoy themselves.

The Role of Design

The sustainability of any city is rooted to the natural conditions and constraints that underlie that city—these technical realities are what I call "hard systems." Layered on top of these fundamentals are a series of socially, politically, and culturally derived "soft systems." These layered "soft" and "hard" systems often need to resolve in physical form. The physical form, or design, will often determine the longevity of a piece of built environment. If successful, the design will enable people to make an emotional connection to a place by imbuing it with character, memory, identity, orientation, and individuality. The actual form and content of the design can largely determine the success of regenerated and newly built urban environments.

In their ability to synthesize large amounts of information and then translate a planning exercise into a physical reality, designers act as translators between the wants and needs of a community and the myriad professional consultants who are often tasked to devise a sustainable strategy. We, as designers, are charged with understanding both "hard" and "soft" systems that extend far off our site boundaries, yet still influence the outcome of that particular site. We are asked to come to a physical resolution that not only integrates these systems, but also balances the realities of budgets, politics, and social issues with the community desire to create a public space that, in the end, is much greater than the sum of the parts.

In addition to making sure that the public realm is properly planned to provide many services to the citizens of a city, perhaps even more important is our responsibility, through design, to create a sense of place and to engender a sense of belonging.

As we globalize and become more homogeneous, there is an increasing need to create a new or enhanced identity that differentiates neighborhoods or cities from other neighborhoods and cities. Our practice is often asked to create a "there, there" and establish an identity to add a distinctiveness that may give a city a competitive edge, something of crucial importance to new and regenerating cities.

Public spaces have the potential to not only function as places to sit, recreate, and enjoy, but will serve to create a symbol or image for a particular community. Along with all the other pragmatic requirements is the usually unspoken requirement that the space performs as the "face" of the neighborhood or city. Designers are tasked to decipher how that image might be one that is unique to a particular place, strong enough to create an identity that will be embraced by the public.

Emotional Buy-In

The specifics of the planning and design will play a large factor in whether anything is sustainable over time. It is a false belief that one can achieve sustainability based only on smart technologies and functioning ecosystems. People are part of the environmental equation, and nothing can sustain itself over time if they are not invested in it either intellectually or emotionally. All the smart technologies, appropriate materials, and energy used to build a technologically LEED-rated project or community are not sufficient, simply because they are not designed to fit the spiritual, psychological, and emotional needs of the people who will use them. Good and great design can help to achieve this connection.

Design in itself cannot make cities successful, as cities are a very complex layering of moving parts. However, for a city to function maximally, the design quality of a city's public realm components becomes extremely important. Design quality is a crucial factor in whether a city can reach its fullest potential. A city's public realm landscape needs to be designed to be more than merely functional; there must also be wonderful, inspired, attractive places to live and work for people of all ages, ethnicities, and socioeconomic levels.

A Call to Landscape Architects

Our primary role as landscape architects is to understand and synthesize the vast elements of both "hard" and "soft" systems that operate on and in our urban landscapes, and then give shape, form, and meaning to the built physical environments in which we live collectively. We determine the physical character of the

"To plan a city, everything begins with human behavior, but architects and city planners have lost the ability to handle scale. We now approach the design process in plan, as though everyone experiences the world from the top of a high-rise building. But at eye-level, everything is terrible. This type of planning is a waste of time."

— Jan Gehl, Principal, Gehl Architects, Copenhagen

public realm environment which, in turn, determines whether or not a city is attractive to people, and whether people will choose to live in a city over time.

Design must be appreciated as a crucial factor in sustainability. Ignoring design and its importance in connecting people to place is to miss a crucial step in the creation of a sustainable city. This is where our profession is at its best: in the understanding and synthesis of these complex and multi-faceted social, economic, and environmental systems that interact in and on the ground plane, and to plan and give shape to the ground plane so that people will use and come to cherish the places where they live, work, and play. Our job is to achieve buy-in from our end users, the public, if we are to achieve sustainability at community or city level.

Our most valued role in the future is to be well-informed generalists who are able to understand the interrelationships between multi-fold, complex systems and synthesize the information so the relationships are in balance and respond to a particular place. We must be both master strategists and artists that can translate strategies into culturally valuable places.

We must expand our remit to advocate for densification, and within this goal, our role as landscape architects expands exponentially, as the understanding of all the operative systems, both "hard" and "soft," are our core area of knowledge. We must grasp the task at hand in its expanse and complexities, and become the advocates of sustainability at the urban scale. For as long as we trail behind the architects by "greening" their buildings, we are simply fiddling while Rome burns.

Photo Credits

p 9 Courtesy of Martha Schwartz Partners
p 14 Courtesy of Pontefract Castleford Express
p 16 Courtesy of Martha Schwartz Partners
p 17 Photograph by Damien McGlynn, 2008
p 18 Photograph by Peter Barrow
p 20 Courtesy of The Royal Society of Antiquaries of Ireland
p 22,23 From left to right: Photograph by Peter Barrow; Photograph by Emily Waugh; Courtesy of the Dublin Docklands Development Authority
p 24 Top: Photograph by Damien McGlynn, 2008. All rights reserved. Bottom: Photograph by William Murphy (Infomatique)
p 26 Photograph by Ros Kavanagh (www.roskavanagh.com)
p 28 Courtesy of Martha Schwartz Partners
p 30 Courtesy of Martha Schwartz Partners
p 31 Courtesy of Martha Schwartz Partners
p 32 Photograph by Ros Kavanagh (www.roskavanagh.com)
p34 Andrius Burl ga
p 37 Photograph by William Murphy (Infomatique)
p 38 Courtesy of Martha Schwartz Partners
p 40 Top: Photograph by Tom Wexler. Projections by KMA (www.kma.uk). Bottom: Photograph by William Murphy (Infomatique)
p 42 Photograph by Ros Kavanagh (www.roskavanagh.com)
p 44 Photograph by David Birchall (www.silverstreamphotography.co.uk)
p 46 Courtesy of Martha Schwartz Partners
p 48 Courtesy of Manchester Archives and Local Studies
p 50 Photograph by Pete Birkenshaw (BinaryApe)
p 51 Left: Photograph by René C. Nielsen (Shevy) Right: Photograph by pit-yacker
p 52 Courtesy of Martha Schwartz Partners
p 54 Courtesy of Martha Schwartz Partners
p 55 Courtesy of Martha Schwartz Partners
p 58 Courtesy of Martha Schwartz Partners
p 60 Courtesy of Martha Schwartz Partners
p 61 Photograph by Emily Waugh
p 62 Clockwise from left: Photograph by Paul Shaw (perplexed); Courtesy of Martha Schwartz Partners; Photograph by Paul Shaw (perplexed); Photograph by Ollie Sammons
p 64 Copyright Joseph McGarraghy, Prestwich, Manchester
p 65 Uploaded by Rudget
p 66 Courtesy of Martha Schwartz Partners
p 68 Photograph by David Cowlard
p 70 Top: Photograph by Matt Brown (Matt From London) Bottom: Courtesy of London SE1 Community Website
p 73 Photograph by Nick (nicksarebi)
p 74 Photograph by king_david_uk
p 76 Courtesy of Martha Schwartz Partners
p 78 Courtesy of Martha Schwartz Partners
p 79 Courtesy of Martha Schwartz Partners
p 80 Courtesy of Martha Schwartz Partners
p 82 Courtesy of Martha Schwartz Partners
p 83 Courtesy of Martha Schwartz Partners
p 84 Top: Courtesy of Martha Schwartz Partners. Bottom: Photograph by David Cowlard
p 85 Courtesy of Martha Schwartz Partners
p 86 Courtesy of Martha Schwartz Partners
p 87 Courtesy of Martha Schwartz Partners
p 88 Courtesy of Martha Schwartz Partners
p 90 Courtesy of Pontefract Castleford Express
p 92 Photograph by Jack Hulme, copyright of Wakefield Council
p94 Photograph by Jack Hulme, copyright of

Wakefield Council
p 95 Courtesy of Martha Schwartz Partners
p 96 Courtesy of Martha Schwartz Partners
p 98 Top: Photograph by Jack Hulme, copyright of Wakefield Council Bottom: Courtesy of Martha Schwartz Partners
p 99 Top: Courtesy of Castleford Heritage Trust. Bottom: Courtesy of Martha Schwartz Partners
p 100 Courtesy of Martha Schwartz Partners
p 101 Courtesy of Castleford Heritage Trust
p 104 Courtesy of Martha Schwartz Partners
p 105 Courtesy of Martha Schwartz Partners
p 106 Courtesy of Castleford Heritage Trust
p 108 Courtesy of Martha Schwartz Partners
p 110,111 Courtesy of Martha Schwartz Partners
p 112 Courtesy of Martha Schwartz Partners (photograph by Bill Smith)
p 114 Courtesy of Hank McNeil (photograph by Jennifer Croney)
p 116 Courtesy of Hank McNeil (photograph by Jennifer Croney)
p 120 Courtesy of Martha Schwartz Partners (photograph by Bill Smith)
p 121 Top: Courtesy of Hank McNeil (photograph by Jennifer Croney) Bottom: Courtesy of Martha Schwartz Partners (photograph by Bill Smith)
p 122 Courtesy of Martha Schwartz Partners (photograph by Bill Smith)
p 124 Courtesy of Martha Schwartz Partners
p 127 Courtesy of Martha Schwartz Partners
p 128 Courtesy of Martha Schwartz Partners
p 129 Courtesy of Martha Schwartz Partners (photograph by Bill Smith)
p 130 Courtesy of Martha Schwartz Partners
p 131 Courtesy of Martha Schwartz Partners
p 132 Courtesy of Martha Schwartz Partners
p 134 Courtesy of Martha Schwartz Partners
p 136 Photograph by Laurent Gauthier (loranger)
p 138 Photograph by Ra'ike
p 139 Photograph by Marc Ryan
p 140 Courtesy of Martha Schwartz Partners
p 141 Courtesy of Martha Schwartz Partners
p 142 Courtesy of Martha Schwartz Partners
p 143 Courtesy of Martha Schwartz Partners
p 144 Courtesy of Martha Schwartz Partners
p 146 Courtesy of Martha Schwartz Partners
p 147 Courtesy of Martha Schwartz Partners
p 148 Courtesy of Martha Schwartz Partners
p 150 Courtesy of Martha Schwartz Partners
p 152 Top: Courtesy of Thunder Bay Public Library (Local History Collection) Thunder Bay, Canada. Bottom: Courtesy of Martha Schwartz Partners
p 154 Courtesy of Martha Schwartz Partners
p 156 Courtesy of Martha Schwartz Partners
p 158,159 Courtesy of Martha Schwartz Partners
p 160,161 Courtesy of Martha Schwartz Partners
p 162,163 Courtesy of Martha Schwartz Partners
p 164 Photograph by Michel Lafrance, Geraldton, Ontario, Canada. P0T 1M0
p 166 Courtesy of Martha Schwartz Partners
p 168 Courtesy of Martha Schwartz Partners
p 174 Photograph by Emily Waugh
p 176 Courtesy of Harvard GSD Studio Participants
p 177 Top: Courtesy of Martha Schwartz Partners. Bottom: Photograph by 3:0 Landschaftsarchitektur – Vienna
p 178 Top: Photographs by 3:0 Landschaftsarchitektur – Vienna

p 180 Google Earth
p 182,183 Courtesy of Porr Solutions
p 184 Courtesy of Martha Schwartz Partners
p 186 Photograph by 3:0 Landschaftsarchitektur – Vienna
p 187 Photograph by 3:0 Landschaftsarchitektur – Vienna
p 188 Photograph by 3:0 Landschaftsarchitektur – Vienna
p 189 Photograph by 3:0 Landschaftsarchitektur – Vienna
p 190 Photograph by 3:0 Landschaftsarchitektur – Vienna
p 192 Courtesy of Martha Schwartz Partners
p 193 Courtesy of Martha Schwartz Partners
p 195 All images courtesy of Martha Schwartz Partners except for center image Courtesy of Monte Laa
p 196 Top: Photograph by 3:0 Landschaftsarchitektur – Vienna
p 197 Photograph by 3:0 Landschaftsarchitektur – Vienna
pp 198 – 210 Courtesy of Harvard GSD Studio Participants
p 218 -237 Courtesy of Martha Schwartz Partners
p 238 – Google Earth
p 240 – Courtesy of Martha Schwartz Partners
p 241 – Courtesy of Martha Schwartz Partners/SOM
p 242 Top: Courtesy of Martha Schwartz Partners/SOM. Bottom: Courtesy of SOM.
p 244 Courtesy of SOM
p 246 Left: Photograph by Imre Solt. Right: Photograph by Bashar Al-Ba'noon (radiant guy)
p 247 Courtesy of SOM
p 248 Courtesy of Martha Schwartz Partners/SOM
p 250 Courtesy of Martha Schwartz Partners
p 252 Courtesy of Martha Schwartz Partners
p 255 Courtesy of Martha Schwartz Partners
p 256 Courtesy of Martha Schwartz Partners
p 258 Courtesy of Martha Schwartz Partners
p 260 Photograph by Tim Roberts Photography, Mesa, Arizona
p 262 Postcard photographed by Ethan (SportSuburban)
p 263 Courtesy of Martha Schwartz Partners
p 264 Courtesy of Martha Schwartz Partners
p 265 Courtesy of Martha Schwartz Partners
p 266 Courtesy of Martha Schwartz Partners
p 267 Courtesy of Martha Schwartz Partners
p 268 Courtesy of Martha Schwartz Partners
p 269 Courtesy of Martha Schwartz Partners
p 270 Courtesy of Martha Schwartz Partners
p 271 Courtesy of Martha Schwartz Partners
p 272 Courtesy of Martha Schwartz Partners
p 274-275 Top row from left: Photograph by Nicole Webb (Nichole Photog); Gilbert, Arizona; Photograph by Jodi Salvi; Courtesy of Martha Schwartz Partners. Middle row from left: Courtesy of Martha Schwartz Partners; Copyright David Orr Photography (www.davidorrphotography.com); Courtesy of Martha Schwartz Partners. Bottom row from left: Photograph by Diana Elizabeth Photography; Photograph by Dorothy Fetter of Dorothy Tess Photography; Photograph by Dorothy Fetter of Dorothy Tess Photography; Photograph by Ashleigh Butler Photography
p 277 Courtesy of Martha Schwartz Partners

Project Credits

01 Grand Canal Square, Dublin Ireland
Martha Schwartz, Shauna Gillies-Smith, Donald Sharp, Friederike Huth, John Pegg, Paula Craft, Jessica Canfield, Christian Weier, Jay Rohrer, Sue Bailey, Isabel Zempel, Amit Arya, Christian Janssen, Courtney Pope, Heather Ring, James Cogliano, James Vincent, Joe Ficociello, Laura Knosp, Maria Bellalta, Matt Fougerat, Rebecca Verner, Thomas Oles, Mara Todorovic, Wileen Kao

In collaboration with:
Associate Landscape Architects: Tiros Resources
Engineers: Nicholas O'Dwyer Limited, Omar Consulting Engineers
Lighting Designer: Speirs and Major Associates
Pavilion Designer: Grant Studio Architects

02 Exchange Square, Manchester, England
Martha Schwartz, Shauna Gillies-Smith, Donald Sharp, Paula Meijerink, Lital Szmuk Fabian, Tricia Bales, Wes Michaels, Evelyn Bergaila, Scott Carmen, Raphael Justewicz, Francesca Levaggi, Michael Wasser, James Lord, Michael Blier, Roderick Wyllie

In collaboration with: Urban Solutions Manchester

03 St. Mary's Churchyard, London, England
Martha Schwartz, Edda Ostertag, Friederike Huth, Susan Bailey, Annghi Tran, Deborah Nagan, Daniel Rea, Chris Bailey, C Kwong Hang Wong, Christian Weier, Claudia Stolte, Jaco Nel, John Pegg, Julian Bolleter, Laurie Preble, Leighton Pace, Marcus Shields, Matt Fougerat, Nigel Thorne, Paula Craft, Simone Marsh

In collaboration with:
Quantity surveyor & CDM co-coordinator: Davis Langdon LLP
Clerk of works: PDM Consultants
Transport Engineers: JMP Consulting
Contractor: Blakedown Landscapes SE
Structural Engineers: Glanville Consultants

04 Village Green, Fryston, England
Martha Schwartz, John Pegg, Matt Fougerat, Paula Craft, R. Luna, Sebastian Koepf, Steve Tycz, Trevor Lee, Angela Lim, Han Song Lee, Humberto Panti Garza, Isabel Zempel, Christian Bender, Christian Weier, David Mendelson, Donald Booth, Meredith Redford, Sam Fleischmann

In collaboration with: Local Landscape Architects: BDP

05 Winslow Farms Conservancy, Winslow, USA
Martha Schwartz, Kathryn Drinkhouse, Michael Blier, Kevin Conger, Paula Meijerink, Evelyn Bergaila, Lital Szmuk-Fabian, Melanie Mignault, Michel Langevin

In collaboration with:
Client: Hank McNeil
Ecologist: David Smart
Engineering and Earth Moving: Richard Pierson
Financing: Brett Senior
Tom Carty
Ed McGlinchey
Jennifer Chernak
Cole and Calder McNeil

06 Geraldton Tailings Landscape, Geraldton, Canada
Martha Schwartz, Lital Szmuk Fabian, James Lord, Tricia Bales, Shauna Gillies-Smith

In collaboration with: Cook Engineering (Paul Brugger)

07 Power Lines, Gelsenkirchen, Germany
Martha Schwartz, Markus Jatsch

In collaboration with: M. Stricker

08 Central Park Monte Laa, Vienna, Austria
Martha Schwartz, Isabel Zempel, Nicole Gaenzler, France Cormier, Paula Meijerink, Sari Weissman, Friederike Huth, Nora Libertun

In collaboration with:
Master Plan Architect: Atelier Albert Wimmer
Local Landscape Architect:
3:0 Landschaftsarchitektur – Vienna

09 Abu Dhabi Corniche Beach, Abu Dhabi, UAE
Martha Schwartz, Matthew Getch, Peter Piet, Deborah Nagan, Nigel Koch, Ceylan Belek, Mattia Gambardella, Chris Wong, Rebecca Orr, Elizabeth Leidy, Donald Sharp, Evelyn Bergaila, Jaco Nel, Jennifer McKenzie, Kai Fu, Laurie Preble, Mike Brizell, Nancy Morgan, Robyn Perkins, Tao Jiang

In collaboration with:
Client: Abu Dhabi Urban Planning Council (UPC)
Client: Davis Langdon (AECOM)
Architect: Jatsch Laux Architects
Retail Consultant: Jones Lang LaSalle
Engineer: KEO International Consultants

10 Jumeirah Gardens, Dubai, UAE
Martha Schwartz, Donald Sharp, Jake Walker, Dan Gass, Allison Dailey, Maria Bellalta, Hirotsugu Tsuchiya, Dong Zhang, Stella Pantelia, Ziying Tang, Amit Arya, Buvana Murali, Chester Nielsen, Courtney Pope, Darren Sears, Payam Ostovar, Alexandra Steed, Fabiana Alvear, Jaco Nel, Jae Yoon Lee, James Cogliano, Jong Hyun Baek, Laurie Preblem, Peter Piet, SiSi Sun, Toshihiko Karato, Victor Kusmin

In collaboration with: SOM

11 Mesa Arts Center, Mesa, Arizona
Martha Schwartz, Shauna Gillies-Smith, Paula Meijerink, Roy Fabian, Donald Sharp, France Cormier, Kristina Patterson, Krystal England, Sari Weissman, Michael Glueck, Nicole Gaenzler, Lital Szmuk Fabian, Michael Kilkelly, Nate Trevethan, Wes Michaels, Susan Ornelas, Tricia Bales, Albert Jacob, Evelyn Bergaila, Letitia Tormay, John Spielberger, Steve Foster, Trevor Lee

In collaboration with:
Local Landscape Architect: Design Workshop
Technical Landscape Consultant: Ryan Associates
Design Architect: Boora Architects- Bud Oringdulph and Michael Tingley
Executive Architect: DWL Architects + Planners, Inc.
Local Landscape Architect: Design Workshop
Technical Landscape Consultant: Ryan Associates
Fountain Designer: Dan Euser / Waterarchitecture
Project Manager: Kitchell

Endnotes

Grand Canal Square

[1] "The History Of Dublin." *Wikipedia*. Online at http://en.wikipedia.org/wiki/History_of_Dublin, accessed March 14, 2011.
[2] Ibid.

Exchange Square

[1] Ian Taylor, Karen Evans, Penny Fraser, eds, *A Tale of Two Cities: Global Change, Local Feeling, and Everyday Life in the North of England: A Study in Manchester and Sheffield* (Routledge, 1996), 61
[2] Euan Kellie. Author of *Rebuilding Manchester*
[3] "Manchester City Centre." *Wikipedia*. Online at http://en.wikipedia.org/wiki/Manchester_city_centre, accessed April 6, 2011.

St. Mary's Churchyard

[1] "Elephant and Castle." *London SE1 Community Website*. Online at http://www.london-se1.co.uk/areas/elephant.html, accessed March 14, 2011.

IBA

[1] Claudia Schreckenbach, Christel Teschner, "I B A Emscher Park – A Beacon Approach, Dealing With Shrinking Cities In Germany." Online at www.cudc.kent.edu/d-Service-Learning/Mahoning/Emscher.pdf, accessed March 27, 2011.
[2] "Ruhr." *Wikipedia*. Online at http://en.wikipedia.org/wiki/Ruhr_region#World_War_II, accessed March 26, 2011
[3] Schreckenbach and Tecschner

Geraldton Tailings Landscape

[1] Edgar J. Lavoie. "Some Local History." Online at http://www.greenstone.ca/DiscoverGreenstone/Interesting-Bits/LocalHistoryClips.aspx, accessed March 25 2011.
[2] *Kenogamisis Region Tourist Attraction Project Report*
[3] Ibid.

Central Park Monte Laa

[1] Michael Jandl and Albert Kraler, "Austria: A Country of Immigration?" Online at http://www.migrationinformation.org/Profiles/display.cfm?id=105, accessed March 22, 2011.
[2] Gerhard Hatz and Heinz Fassmann, György Enyedi and Zoltán Kovács (eds.), published in 2006: *Social Changes and Social Sustainability in Historical Urban Centres: The Case of Central Europe*. Pecs. Hungarian Academy of Sciences. Centre for Regional Studies. p.218-236.

Mesa Arts Center

[1] Hait, Pam Day Trips from Phoenix, Tucson, and Flagstaff, 9th Edition: *Getaway Ideas for the Local Traveler* (Morris Book Publishing, 2007)

Acknowledgments

We would like to thank everyone who has contributed their time, knowledge, resources, words, and images to this project— without your hard work and generosity this book would not exist.

We would especially like to say thank you to:

Martha Schwartz for opening up your life and your work for this publication and for devoting so much of your personal time and efforts to the project.

The people at Martha Schwartz Partners who contributed long-term support of the office and who enabled us to produce the work that made this book worth doing. Special thanks to Nancy Morgan, Evelyn Bergaila, Don Sharp, Shauna Gillies-Smith, Matt Getch, Jake Walker, Dan Gass and Allison Dailey. And many thanks to those within MSP who assisted in the organization of the book: Ceylan Belek, Raoul Bukor, David May, Jennifer McKenzie, Edda Ostertag, Matthew Roark, Faun Schwartz, and Abhishek Sharma.
Jan Gehl, Ken Livingstone, Beth Meyer, and Charles Waldheim for generously sharing your time and knowledge with us.

Everyone who took time out of their incredibly busy lives to be interviewed and to share critical information with us: Jon Abbott, Johannes Altenburg, Betty Ashe, Edward Bird, Paul Brugger, John Doorly, Alison Drake, Joanie Flatt, Nora Gesellmann, Andy Golding, Euan Kellie, Sir Richard Leese, Robert Luger, Lee Macodrum, John McDonough, John McLaughlin, Edward McGlinchy, Hank McNeil, Chris Munro, Shane O'Toole, Otto Raschauer, Rebecca Towers, Albert Wimmer, and Daniel Zimmerman

Our research and image collection team: Nina Chase, Justin Cheung, and Brett Snyder

The design team at Studio:Blackwell for making the book so beautiful.

Everyone at ORO Editions and especially to Gordon Goff and Usana Shadday for curating as smooth a process as possible.

And finally, a very special note to those of you who, throughout this project and beyond, continue to offer your unending support, help, and advice: Marc Ryan, Katy Waugh, and Paul Nakazawa, there is not a thank you big enough for your efforts.

ORO *editions*
Publishers of Architecture, Art, and Design
Gordon Goff: Publisher

USA, ASIA, EUROPE, MIDDLE EAST
www.oroeditions.com
info@oroeditions.com

ISBN: 978-1-9359350-3-2

ORO editions has made every effort to minimize the overall carbon footprint of this project. As part of this goal, ORO editions, in association with Global ReLeaf, have arranged to plant two trees for each and every tree used in the manufacturing of the paper produced for this book. Global ReLeaf is an international campaign run by American Forests, the nation's oldest nonprofit conservation organization. Global ReLeaf is American Forests' education and action program that helps individuals, organizations, agencies, and corporations improve the local and global environment by planting and caring for trees.

Graphic Design: Studio Blackwell
Production Manager: Usana Shadday
Production Assistance: Gabriel Ely
Project Coordinator: Christy LaFaver
Edited by: Emily Waugh

Color Separations and Printing: ORO Group Ltd.
Printed in China.

Text printed using offset sheetfed printing process in 4 color on 157gsm premium matt art paper with an off-line gloss acqueous spot varnish applied to all photographs.

ORO editions has made every effort to minimize the overall carbon footprint of this project. As part of this goal, ORO editions, in association with Global ReLeaf, have arranged to plant two trees for each and every tree used in the manufacturing of the paper produced for this book. Global ReLeaf is an international campaign run by American Forests, the nation's oldest nonprofit conservation organization. Global ReLeaf is American Forests' education and action program that helps individuals, organizations, agencies, and corporations improve the local and global environment by planting and caring for trees.

International Distribution
www.oroeditions.com

OLDNAVY